Mastering Social Media Mining with R

Extract valuable data from social media sites and make better business decisions using R

Sharan Kumar Ravindran

Vikram Garg

BIRMINGHAM - MUMBAI

Mastering Social Media Mining with R

First published: September 2015

Production reference: 1180915

Published by Packt Publishing Ltd.
Livery Place
35 Livery Street
Birmingham B3 2PB, UK.

ISBN 978-1-78439-631-2

www.packtpub.com

Credits

Authors
Sharan Kumar Ravindran

Vikram Garg

Reviewers
Richard Iannone

Hasan Kurban

Mahbubul Majumder

Haichuan Wang

Commissioning Editor
Pramila Balan

Acquisition Editor
Rahul Nair

Content Development Editor
Susmita Sabat

Technical Editor
Manali Gonsalves

Copy Editor
Roshni Banerjee

Project Coordinator
Milton Dsouza

Proofreader
Safis Editing

Indexer
Priya Sane

Graphics
Sheetal Aute

Disha Haria

Production Coordinator
Shantanu N. Zagade

Cover Work
Shantanu N. Zagade

About the Authors

Sharan Kumar Ravindran is a data scientist with over five years of experience. He is currently working for a leading e-commerce company in India. His primary interests lie in statistics and machine learning, and he has worked with customers from Europe and the U.S. in the e-commerce and IoT domains.

He holds an MBA degree with specialization in marketing and business analysis. He conducts workshops for Anna University to train their staff, research scholars, and volunteers in analytics.

In addition to coauthoring *Social Media Mining with R*, he has also reviewed *R Data Visualization Cookbook*. He maintains a website, www.rsharankumar.com, with links to his social profiles and blog.

I would like to thank the R community for their generous contributions.

I am grateful to Mr. Derick Jose for the inspiration and opportunities given to me.

I would like to thank all my friends, colleagues, and family members, without whom I wouldn't have learned as much.

I would like to thank my dad and brother-in-law for all their support and also helping me in proofreading and testing.

I would like to thank my wife, Aishwarya, and my sister, Saranya, for the constant motivation, and also my son, Rithik, and niece, Shravani, who make every day of mine joyful and fulfilling.

Most of all, I would like to thank my mother for always believing in me.

Vikram Garg (@vikram_garg) is a senior analytical engineer at a Big Data organization. He is passionate about applying machine learning approaches to any given domain and creating technology to amplify human intelligence. He completed his graduation in computer science and electrical engineering from IIT, Delhi. When he is not solving hard problems, he can be found playing tennis or in a swimming pool.

I would like to dedicate all my books to my parents and my brother. Without whom I am no one.

About the Reviewers

Richard Iannone is an R enthusiast and a very simple person. Those who know him (and know him well) know that this is indeed true. He has authored many R packages that have achieved great success. Those who have reviewed the code know that it possesses a *je ne sais quoi* essence to it. In any case, the code coverage is quite adequate (thanks to the many "test parties" he held), and he often offers builds that pass muster according to Travis CI.

Although he has a tendency toward modesty, others have remarked that he's just a straight shooter with upper management written all over him. You know what, we couldn't agree more. We bet you'll hear a *lot more* about him in the near future.

Hasan Kurban is a PhD candidate from the School of Informatics and Computing at Indiana University, Bloomington. He is majoring in Computer Science and minoring in Statistics. His main fields of interest are Data Mining, Machine Learning, Data Science, and Statistics. He also received his master's degree in Computer Science from Indiana University, Bloomington, in 2012. You can contact him at hakurban@indiana.edu.

Mahbubul Majumder is an assistant professor of statistics in the Department of Mathematics, the University of Nebraska at Omaha (UNO). He earned his PhD in statistics with specialization in data visualization and visual statistical inference from Iowa State University. He had the opportunity to work with some industries dealing with data and creating data products. His research interests include exploratory data analysis, data visualization, and statistical modeling. He teaches data science and he is currently developing a data science program for UNO.

Haichuan Wang holds a PhD degree in computer science from the University of Illinois at Urbana-Champaign. He has worked extensively in the field of programming languages and on runtime systems, and he worked in the R language and GNU-R system for a few years. He has also worked in the machine learning and pattern recognition fields. He is passionate about bringing R into parallel and distributed computing domains to handle massive data processing.

I'd like to thank Bo for always loving and supporting me.

I'd also like to thank my PhD advisors, Prof. Padua and Dr. Wu, and my MS advisor, Prof. Zhang, who triggered my interest in this field and guided me throughout this journey.

www.PacktPub.com

Support files, eBooks, discount offers, and more

For support files and downloads related to your book, please visit www.PacktPub.com.

Did you know that Packt offers eBook versions of every book published, with PDF and ePub files available? You can upgrade to the eBook version at www.PacktPub.com and as a print book customer, you are entitled to a discount on the eBook copy. Get in touch with us at service@packtpub.com for more details.

At www.PacktPub.com, you can also read a collection of free technical articles, sign up for a range of free newsletters and receive exclusive discounts and offers on Packt books and eBooks.

https://www2.packtpub.com/books/subscription/packtlib

Do you need instant solutions to your IT questions? PacktLib is Packt's online digital book library. Here, you can search, access, and read Packt's entire library of books.

Why subscribe?

- Fully searchable across every book published by Packt
- Copy and paste, print, and bookmark content
- On demand and accessible via a web browser

Free access for Packt account holders

If you have an account with Packt at www.PacktPub.com, you can use this to access PacktLib today and view 9 entirely free books. Simply use your login credentials for immediate access.

Table of Contents

Preface

In recent times, the popularity of social media has grown exponentially and is increasingly being used as a channel for mass communication, such that the brands consider it as a medium of promotion and people largely use it for content sharing. With the increase in the number of users online, the data generated has increased many folds, bringing in the huge scope for gaining insights into the untapped gold mine, the social media data.

Mastering Social Media Mining with R will provide you with a detailed step-by-step guide to access the data using R and the APIs of various social media sites, such as Twitter, Facebook, Instagram, GitHub, Foursquare, LinkedIn, Blogger, and a few more networks. Most importantly, this book will provide you detailed explanations of implementation of various use cases using R programming; and by reading this book, you will be ready to embark your journey as an independent social media analyst. This book is structured in such a way that people new to the field of data mining or a seasoned professional can learn to solve powerful business cases with the application of machine learning techniques on the social media data.

What this book covers

Chapter 1, *Fundaments of Mining*, introduces you to the concepts of social media mining, various social media platforms, generic processes involved in accessing and processing the data, and techniques that can be implemented, as well as the importance, challenges, and applications of social media mining.

Chapter 2, *Mining Opinions, Exploring Trends, and More with Twitter*, focuses on steps involved in collecting tweets using the Twitter API and solve business cases, such as identifying the trending topics, searching tweets, collecting tweets, processing them, performing sentiment analysis, exploring few business cases based on sentiment analysis, and visualizing the sentiments in the form of word clouds.

Chapter 3, Find Friends on Facebook, discusses the usage of the Facebook API and uses the extracted data to measure click-through rate performance, detect spam messages, implement and explore the concepts of social graphs, and build recommendations using the Apriori algorithm on pages to like.

Chapter 4, Finding Popular Photos on Instagram, helps you understand the procedure involved in pulling the data using the Instagram API and helps you extract the popular personalities and destinations, building different types of clusters, and implementing recommendation engine based on the user-based collaborative filtering approach.

Chapter 5, Let's Build Software with GitHub, teaches you to use the GitHub API from R and also helps you understand the ways in which you can get the solutions to business questions by performing graphical and nongraphical exploration data analysis, which includes some basic charts, trend analysis, heat maps, scatter plots, and much more.

Chapter 6, More Social Media Websites, helps you understand the functioning of APIs of various social media websites and covers the business cases that can be solved.

What you need for this book

In order to make your learning efficient, you need to have a computer with either Windows, Mac, or Ubuntu.

You need to download R to execute the codes mentioned in this book. You can download and install R using the CRAN website available at http://cran.r-project.org/. All the codes are written using RStudio. RStudio is an integrated development environment for R and can be downloaded from http://www.rstudio.com/products/rstudio/.

In order to access the APIs of the social media, it will be necessary to create an app and follow certain instructions. All of these procedures are explained in their respective chapters.

Who this book is for

Mastering Social Media Mining with R is intended for those who have basic knowledge of R in terms of its libraries and are aware of different machine learning techniques, or if you are a data analyst and interested in mining social media data; however, there is no need to have any prior knowledge of the usage of APIs of social media websites. This book will make you master in getting the required social media data and transforming them into actions resulting in improved business values.

Conventions

In this book, you will find a number of text styles that distinguish between different kinds of information. Here are some examples of these styles and an explanation of their meaning.

Code words in text, database table names, folder names, filenames, file extensions, pathnames, dummy URLs, user input, and Twitter handles are shown as follows: "We can include other contexts through the use of the include directive."

A block of code is set as follows:

```
[default]
post_id<- head(page$id, n = 100)
head(post_id, n=10)
post_id<- as.matrix(post_id)
```

Any command-line input or output is written as follows:

```
# Location (Country)
```

New terms and **important words** are shown in bold. Words that you see on the screen, for example, in menus or dialog boxes, appear in the text like this: "Clicking the **Next** button moves you to the next screen."

 Exercise to be tried by the readers and notes appear in a box like this.

Reader feedback

Feedback from our readers is always welcome. Let us know what you think about this book—what you liked or disliked. Reader feedback is important for us as it helps us develop titles that you will really get the most out of.

To send us general feedback, simply e-mail feedback@packtpub.com, and mention the book's title in the subject of your message.

If there is a topic that you have expertise in and you are interested in either writing or contributing to a book, see our author guide at www.packtpub.com/authors.

Customer support

Now that you are the proud owner of a Packt book, we have a number of things to help you to get the most from your purchase.

Downloading the example code

You can download the example code files from your account at http://www.packtpub.com for all the Packt Publishing books you have purchased. If you purchased this book elsewhere, you can visit http://www.packtpub.com/support and register to have the files e-mailed directly to you.

Errata

Although we have taken every care to ensure the accuracy of our content, mistakes do happen. If you find a mistake in one of our books—maybe a mistake in the text or the code—we would be grateful if you could report this to us. By doing so, you can save other readers from frustration and help us improve subsequent versions of this book. If you find any errata, please report them by visiting http://www.packtpub.com/submit-errata, selecting your book, clicking on the **Errata Submission Form** link, and entering the details of your errata. Once your errata are verified, your submission will be accepted and the errata will be uploaded to our website or added to any list of existing errata under the Errata section of that title.

To view the previously submitted errata, go to https://www.packtpub.com/books/content/support and enter the name of the book in the search field. The required information will appear under the **Errata** section.

Piracy

Piracy of copyrighted material on the Internet is an ongoing problem across all media. At Packt, we take the protection of our copyright and licenses very seriously. If you come across any illegal copies of our works in any form on the Internet, please provide us with the location address or website name immediately so that we can pursue a remedy.

Please contact us at copyright@packtpub.com with a link to the suspected pirated material.

We appreciate your help in protecting our authors and our ability to bring you valuable content.

Questions

If you have a problem with any aspect of this book, you can contact us at questions@packtpub.com, and we will do our best to address the problem.

1
Fundamentals of Mining

Our approach in this book will be to use statistics and social science theory to mine social media and we'll use R as our base programming language. We will walk you through many important and recent developments in the field of social media. We'll cover advanced topics such as **Open Authorization (OAuth)**, Twitter's OAuth API, Facebook's graph API, and so on, along with some interesting references and resources. It is assumed that the target audience has a basic understanding of R, along with basic concepts of social sciences.

In this chapter, we will cover the following topics:

- Importance of social media mining
- Basics of social media mining
- Social media mining techniques
- Basic data mining algorithms
- Opinion mining
- Social recommendations

Social media and its importance

In simple terms, social media is a way of communication using online tools such as Twitter, Facebook, LinkedIn, and so on. Andreas Kaplan and Michael Haenlein define social media as follows:

> "A group of Internet-based applications that build on the ideological and technological foundations of Web 2.0 and that allow the creation and exchange of user-generated content".

Social media spans lots of Internet-based platforms that facilitate human emotions such as:

- Networking, for example, Facebook, LinkedIn, and so on
- Micro blogging, for example, Twitter, Tumblr, and so on
- Photo sharing, for example, Instagram, Flickr, and so on
- Video sharing, for example, YouTube, Vimeo, and so on
- Stack exchanging, for example, Stack Overflow, Github, and so on
- Instant messaging, for example, Whatsapp, Hike, and so on

The traditional media such as radio, newspaper, or television, facilitates one-way communication with a limited scope of reach and usability. Though the audience can interact (two-way communication) with these channels, particularly radio, the quality and frequency of such communications are very limited. On the other hand, Internet-based social media offers multi-way communication with features such as immediacy and permanence. It is important to understand all the aspects of social media today because real customers are using it.

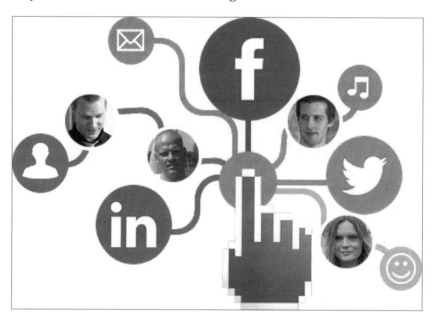

Today's corporate marketing departments are maturing in understanding the promise or the impact of social media. In the early years, social media was perceived as yet another broadcasting medium for publishing banner advertisements into the world. Unfortunately, many still believe this to be the only use of social media. While it's not deniable that social media is a great tool for banner advertisements in terms of cost and reach, it's not limited to that. There is another use of social media that can turn out to be more influential in the long term. Businesses need to heed to the opinion of the consumer by mining social networks. By gathering information on the opinions of consumers, they can understand current and potential customers' outlook, and such informative data can guide business decisions, in the long run, influencing the fate of any business.

Current **customer relationship management** (**CRM**) systems create consumer profiles to help with marketing judgments using a mixture of demographics, past buying patterns, and other prior actions. These methods basically empower companies to keep a close eye on their consumers. The customer data available via communities such as LinkedIn or Facebook is quite detailed. A financial business with access to such data would not only know the intricate details of a customer, but also the interests of the customer, and evidence that might be beneficial in preparation of future marketing plans. Every minute of every day, Facebook, Twitter, LinkedIn, and other online communities generate enormous amounts of this data. If it could be mined, it might work like a real-time CRM, persistently revealing new trends and opportunities.

Various social media platforms

Social media is not restricted to email or chat or media sharing; it is collection of a larger group of content generating platforms such as:

- Blogs
- Micro blogs
- Social news
- Social bookmarking
- Professional groups
- Community-based questions and answers
- Wikis

Social media mining

In simple terms, social media mining is a *systematic analysis of information generated from social media*. It becomes necessary to tap into this enormous social media data with the help of today's technology, which is not without its challenges. Data stream is a prime example of Big Data. Dealing with data sets measured in petabytes is challenging, and things like signal-to-noise ratio need to be taken into consideration. It is estimated that around 20 percent of such social media data streams contain relevant information.

The set of tools and techniques, which are used to mine such information, are collectively called Data mining technique and in the context of social media it's called **social media mining (SMM)**. SMM can generate insights about how much someone is influencing others on the Web. SMM can help businesses identify the pain points of its customer in real time. In turn, this can be used for proactive planning. Identification of potential customers is a very important problem every business has been trying to solve for ages. SMMs can help us identify the potential customers based on their online activities and based on their friend's online activities. There has been a lot of research in multiple disciplines of social media:

- Why does social media mining matter?
- If you can measure it, you can improve it
- Modeling behavior
- Predictive analysis
- Recommending content

Challenges for social media mining

Social media mining is currently in a stage of infancy, and its practitioners are learning and developing new approaches. Social media mining draws its roots from many fields, such as statistics, machine learning, information retrieval, pattern recognition, and bioinformatics. The parent fields themselves are not without their challenges. The sheer amount of data being generated daily is staggering, but current techniques allow for novel data mining solutions and scalable computational models with help from the fundamental concepts and theories and algorithms.

In social media theory, people are considered to be the basic building blocks of a world created on the grounds provided by the social media. The measurements of the interactions between these building blocks and other entities such as sites, networks, content, and so on leads to the discovery of human nature. The knowledge gained via these measurements constitutes the soul of the social worlds. Finding the insights from this data where social relationships play a critical role can be termed as the mining of social media data. This problem not only has to face the basic data mining challenges but also those that emerge because of the social-relationship aspect. We have listed down some of the important challenges here:

- **Big Data**: Should we use the *taste* of a friend of a friend of the person of interest, who has studied at one particular college and whose hometown was one particular city to recommend something to the person of the interest? In some applications, this might be overkill and in others this information could lead to a very small but differentiating performance increase. The content that can be used in social media data can be very deep. However, this can lead to a problem called *over fitting*, which is well known in the domain of machine learning. Using multiple sources of data can also complicate the overall performance in a similar fashion.

- **Sufficiency**: Should we restrict people to view only the person of interest's alma mater and his/her hometown to recommend something and not use the tastes of his/her friends? Common sense says this is not correct and we may be missing out on something. This is a problem commonly known as *under fitting*. This problem can also arise due to the fact that most social media networks restrict the amount of information that can be accessed in a certain time frame, so sometimes the data is not sufficient enough to generate patterns and/or generate recommendations.

- **Noise removal error**: Preprocessing steps are more or less always required in any application of data mining. These steps not only make the actual application run faster on the cleaned data, but they also improve overall accuracy. Due to all the clutter, which is present in most social data, a large amount of noise is always expected but effectively removing the noise from the data we have is a very tricky business. You can always end up missing some information while trying to remove this noise. Noise by its definition is a subjective quantity and can always be confused; hence, this step can end up introducing more error in pattern recognition.

- **Evaluation dilemma**: Because of the sheer size of social media data, it's not possible to obtain a properly annotated dataset to train a supervised machine-learning algorithm. Without the proper ground truth data, there is no way to judge the accuracy of any off-the-shell classification algorithms. Since there can't be any accuracy measures without the ground truth data, only a clustering (unsupervised machine learning) algorithm can be applied. But the problem is that such algorithms rely heavily on the domain expertise.

Social media mining techniques

We'll go through a few of the standard social media mining techniques available. We will consider examples with Facebook and Twitter as our data sources.

Graph mining

Network graphs make up the dominant data structure and appear, essentially, in all forms of social media data/information. Typically, user communities constitute a group of nodes in such graphs where nodes within the same community or cluster tend to share common features.

Graph mining can be described as *the process of extracting useful knowledge (patterns, outliers and so on.) from a social relationship between the community members can be represented as a graph*. The most influential example of graph mining is **Facebook Graph Search**.

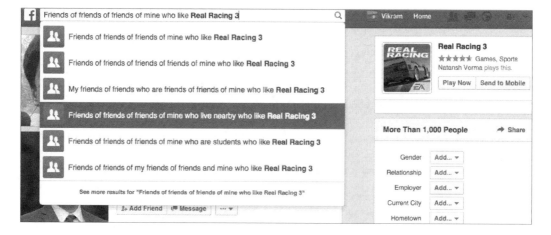

Text mining

Extraction of meaning from unstructured text data present in social media is described as text mining. The primary targets of this type of mining are blogs and micro blogs such as Twitter. It's applicable to other social networks such as Facebook that contain links to posts, blogs, and other news articles.

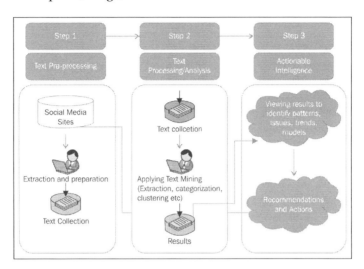

The generic process of social media mining

Any data mining activity follows some generic steps to gain some useful insights from the data. Since social media is the central theme of this book, let's discuss these steps by taking example data from Twitter:

- Getting authentication from the social website
- Data visualization
- Cleaning and preprocessing
- Data modeling using standard algorithms such as opinion mining, clustering, anomaly/spam detection, correlations and segmentations, recommendations
- Result visualization

Getting authentication from the social website – OAuth 2.0

Most social media websites provide API access to their data. To do the mining, we (as a third-party) would need some mechanism to get access to users' data, available on these websites. But the problem is that a user will not share their credentials with anyone due to obvious security reasons. This is where OAuth comes in the picture. According to its home page (http://oauth.net/), OAuth can be defined as follows:

> *An open protocol to allow secure authorization in a simple and standard method from web, mobile and desktop applications.*

To understand it better, let's take an example of Instagram where a user can allow a printing service access to his/her private photographs stored on Instagram's server, without sharing her credentials with the printing service. Instead, they authenticate directly with Instagram, which issues the printing service delegation-specific permissions. The user here is the primary owner of the resource and the printing service is the third-party client. Social media websites such as Instagram, Twitter, and Facebook allow various applications to access user data for various advertisements or recommendations. Almost all cab service applications access user location.

Here's a diagram illustrating the concept:

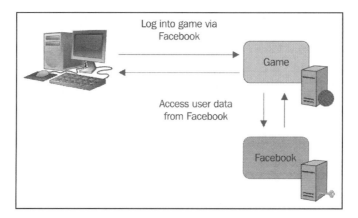

OAuth 2.0 provides various methods in which different levels of authorizations of the various resources can reliably be granted to the requesting client application. One of the most frequently used and most important use cases is the authorization of World Wide Web server data to another World Wide Web server/application.

The following image shows the authentication process:

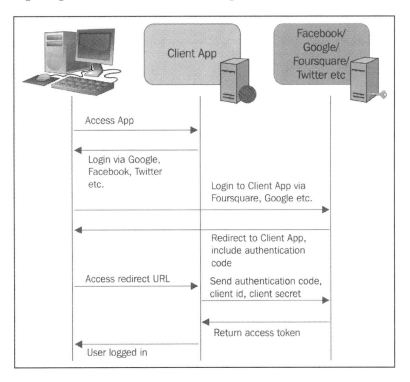

Let's look at the various steps involved:

1. The client accesses the web app with the button **Login via Twitter** (or **Login via LinkedIn** or **Login via Facebook**).

2. This takes the client to an app, which will authenticate it. The client app then asks the user to allow it the access to his/her resources, that is, the profile data. The user needs to accept it to go the next step.

3. The client is then redirected to a redirect link via the authenticating app, which the client app has provided to the authenticating app. Usually, the redirect link is delivered by registering the client app with the authenticating app. The user of the client app also registers the redirect link and at the same time authenticating app also gives the client app with client credentials.

4. Using the redirect link, the client contacts the website in the client app. During this step, a connection between authenticating app and client app is made and the authentication code received in the redirect request parameters. So, an access token is returned by the authenticating app.

Depending on the network, the access provided by the access token can be constrained not only in terms of the information but also the life of the access token itself. As soon as the client app obtains an access token, this access token can be sent to the respective social media organizations, such as Facebook, LinkedIn, Twitter, and so on, to access resources in these servers that are related to the clients who gave permission via the tokens.

Differences between OAuth and OAuth 2.0

Here are some of the major differences:

- More flows in OAuth 2.0 to permit improved support for non-browser based apps
- OAuth 2.0 does not need the client app to have cryptography
- OAuth 2.0 offers much less complicated signatures
- OAuth 2.0 generates *short-lived* access tokens, hence it is more secure
- OAuth 2.0 has a clearer segregation of roles concerning the server responsible for handling user authorization and the server handling OAuth requests

Data visualization R packages

A number of visualization R packages for text data are available as R package. These libraries, based on available data and objective, provide various options varying from simple clusters of words to the one inline with semantic analysis or topic modeling of the corpus. These libraries provide means to better understand text data. In this book, we'll use the following libraries:

The simple word cloud

One of the simplest and most frequently used visualization libraries is the *simple word cloud*. The basic intent to using word cloud is to visualize the weights of the words present. The "wordcloud" R library helps the user get an understanding of weights of a word/term with respect to the tf-idf matrix. The weights are proportional to the size and color of the word you see in the plot. Here's an example of one such simple word cloud based on the corpus created from tweets:

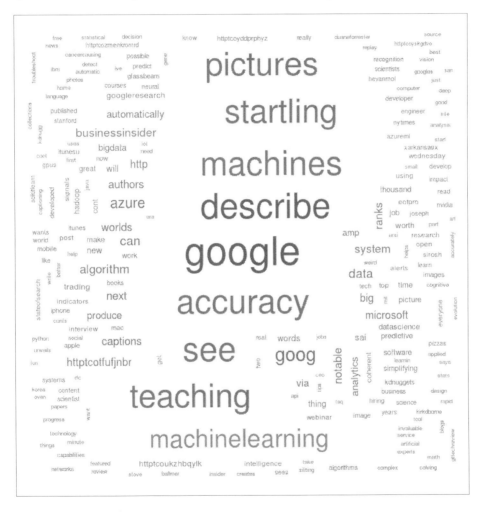

Sentiment analysis Wordcloud

There are R packages that can generate a word cloud similar to the preceding figure, along with the sentiments each word is representing. Such plots are one step ahead of the basic word cloud because they let the user get an understanding of what kind of sentiments are present and why the particular documents (collection of tweets) are of a particular nature (joy, sadness, disgust, love, and so on.). Timothy Jurka developed one such package, which we are going to use. The two main functions of this package are as follows:

- `Classify_emotion`: As the name suggests, the procedure helps the user understand the type of sentiment that is present. This procedure also clusters the words present in the query based on the sentiment and level of emotions that particular word present. A voting-based classification is one the algorithms used in this particular procedure. The Naive Bayes algorithm is also used for more enhanced results. The training dataset used on the above algorithms is from Carlo Strapparava and Alessandro Valitutti. Here's a sample output:

- `Classify_polarity`: This procedure indicates the overall polarity of the emotions (positive or negative). This is, in a way, an extension of the procedure. The training data used here comes from Janyce Wiebe's subjectivity lexicon.

The most commonly used visualization library for Facebook data is *Gephi*. The key difference between Facebook and Twitter is the richness of the profile of a user and the social connections one shares on Facebook. Gephi helps users visualize both of the distinctions in a very pleasant way. It enables a user to understand the impact one Facebook profile has, or could have, over the network. Gephi is highly customizable and user-friendly library. We'll discuss this in *Chapter 3, Find Friends on Facebook*. As a working example, here's the graph representation of a social network of two friends.

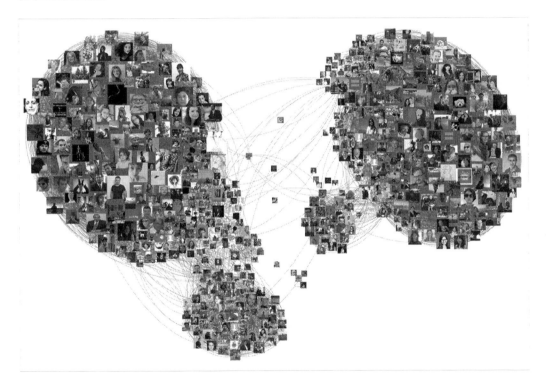

Many more R packages are available to visualize most social media data. For more information, refer to the following links:

- http://rcytoscape.systemsbiology.net/versions/current/index.html
- http://cran.us.r-project.org/web/packages/sna/index.html
- http://statnetproject.org/

Preprocessing and cleaning in R

Preprocessing and cleaning are the very basic and first steps in any data-mining problem. A learning algorithm on a unified and cleaned dataset cannot only run very fast, but can also produce more accurate results. The first steps involve the annotation of target data, in the case of classification problems and understating the feature vector space, to apply an appropriate distance measure for clustering problems. Identification of noise samples and their clean up is a very tricky task but the better it's done, the more accuracy one can expect in the results. As mentioned previously, you need to be careful in cleaning tasks as this can lead to a rejection of good samples. Furthermore, the preprocessing steps need to be a reversible process because at the end of the exercise, the results need to be processed back to the original sample space for it to make sense.

Data modeling – the application of mining algorithms

Let's look at some of the standard mining algorithms.

Opinion mining (sentiment analysis)

In simple words, opinion mining or sentiment analysis is the method in which we try to assess the opinion/sentiment present in the given phrase. The phrase could be any sentence. Though our examples would be English, the sentiment analysis is not limited to any language. Also, the sentence could come from any source—it could be a 140-character tweet, Facebook post/chats, SMSs, and so on. Consider the following examples:

- Visiting to the wonderful places in Europe. Feeling real happy—Positive.
- I love little sunshine in winters, make me feel live—Positive.
- I am stuck in a same place, feeling sad—Negative.
- The cab driver was a nice person. Think many of them are actually good people—Positive.

Sentiment analysis can play a crucial role in understanding the costumer sentiment, which can actually affect the growth of any business. With social media platforms such as Twitter, the meaning of the saying *words are mightier than swords*, has reached a whole new level. In the next chapter, we'll see how the customer sentiments can affect the growth of business. Also, there is nothing like word of mouth marketing, and again social media platforms can help you provide more business via the words of real customers. This field has become so advanced that people have actually predicted the outcomes of major elections based on the sentiments of the voters. Similarly, stock market forecasts are now being generated based on the analysis of customer tweets.

Steps for sentiment analysis

A belief or an opinion or sentiment to a computer can be described as a **quintuple**; that is an object in a five dimensional space, where each axis represents the following:

- O_j: This is the objective (that is, product). It is realized via named entity extraction.
- f_{jk}: This is a feature of O_j. It is assessed using information mining theory
- SO_{ijkl}:This is the sentiment value of the opinion of the opinion holder hi on feature f_{jk} of object o_j at time t_l
- h_i: This is the information miner
- T_i: This is for data extraction

Perform the following steps to get the sentiment value SO_{ijkl}:

1. **Part-of-speech tagging (pos)** means the term in the text (or the sentence) that are marked using a pos-tagger so that it allocates a label to each term, allowing the system to do something with it.

2. We look at **sentiment orientation (SO)** of the patterns we mined. For example, we may have extracted **Remarkable + Handset**, which is, **[JJ] + [NN]** (or adjective trailed by noun). The opposite might be "Awful" for instance. In this phase, the system attempts to position the terms on an emotive scale.

3. The average sentiment orientation of all the terms we gathered is computed. This allows the system to say something like:

    ◦ "Usually individuals like the fresh **Handset**." They recommend it
    ◦ "Usually individuals hate the fresh **Handset**." They don't recommend it

It's not easy to classify sentiments; nonetheless there are various classification algorithms, which have been employed to aid opinion mining. These algorithms vary from simple probabilistic classifiers such as Naïve Bayes (probability classifier that assumes all the features are independent and does not use any prior information) to the more advanced classifiers such as maximum entropy (which uses the prior information to a certain extent.

Many hyperspace classifiers such as **Support Vector Machine (SVM)** and **Neural Networks (NN)** have also been used to correctly classify the sentiments. Between SVM and NN, SVM, in general, works wonders due to the kernel trick.

There are other methods being explored as well. For example, **Anomaly/spam detection or social spammer detection**. Fake profiles created with a malicious intention are known as spam or anomalous profiles. The user who creates such profiles often pretend to be someone they are not and try to perform some inappropriate activity, which can eventually cause problems for the person they were imitating as well as to others. There has been an increase in the number of cases of online bullying, trolling, and so on, which are direct causes of social spamming. We'll show you the various classification algorithms to detect these fake profiles in *Chapter 3, Find Friends on Facebook*.

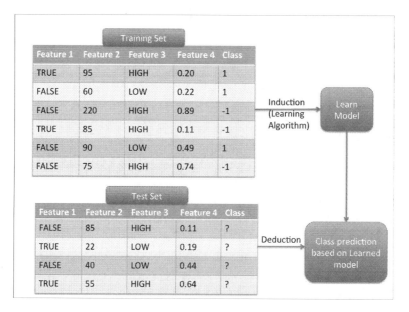

The algorithms we'll use to identify the spam and/or spammers based on a same example datasets, fall under the general class of algorithms known as supervised machine learning algorithms. The example dataset used in these algorithms is called training set. For notational consistency, let's say each ith record in the training set as a pair consists of an input vector represented by x_i and output label represented by y_i. The vector x_i consists of a set of features representative of the ith sample point. The task of such an algorithm is to infer a function f (from a given possible set of functions **F**) which can map the x_i's to the respective y_i's, with high level of accuracy. This function f is sometimes also called a learned/trained model. The process of inferring f, using the training data is called learning. Once the model is trained, we use this learned model with the new records to identify new labels. The ability of such a model/algorithm to correctly identify the new example set (also called test set) labels that differ from the training set, is known as generalization.

There are many algorithms under the class of supervised machine learning algorithms such as the Naïve Bayes classifier, Decision tree classifier, and so on. One such algorithm is SVM. In a two-class (binary) classification problem, an SVM is the maximal margin hyperplane that separate the two classes with the largest possible margin. If there are more than two classes, then multiple SVMs are learned under one-versus-rest or one-versus-one methods; discussing these two methods is beyond the scope of the book.

The following figure illustrates a binary classification by SVM. The red and black dots are part of training data point x_i's, representing the two types of the label y_i. SVM comes with a neat transformation, which can transform the current feature space to a new feature space using various kernels. Discussing the details is beyond the scope of this book.

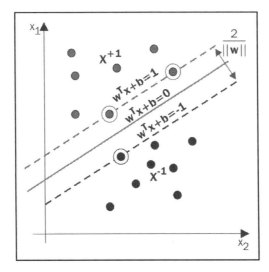

Community detection via clustering

In graph analogy, a community is a set of nodes between which the communications/ interactions are rather more frequent than with those outside the set. From a marketing point of view, community detection become very crucial and has been proven to be very rewarding in terms of **return-of-investments (ROIs)**. For example, travel enthusiasts can be identified on various social media websites based on their visited places, posts, comments, tweets, and so on. If such segmentation can be done, then selling them some product related to travel (such as a handheld compass, travel pillow, global alarm clock, binoculars, slim digital camera, noise-cancelling headphones, and so on) would stand a higher chance of purchase. Hence, with a focused marketing effort, the business can get more ROIs.

While spam detection is a supervised machine-learning task, community detection or clustering falls under the class of unsupervised learning algorithms. Social media offers two types of communities. Some are explicitly created groups with people of common location, hobbies, or occupation. There are several other people who might not be connected to such groups. Identification of these people is a clustering task. This is performed based on their interaction (for example, they mentioned a common thing in their comments/posts/tweets) as features sets (x_i's) and without label information (as in the case of supervised machine learning algorithms). These features are passed to various unsupervised machine learning algorithms to find the commonalities and hence the communities. Many algorithms also provide the extent/degree/affinity score with which a particular person belongs to a specific community.

There are many algorithms and techniques proposed in academia that we'll discuss in detail in the following chapters. Basically, these methods are based on calculation of the influence on the link between various edges (people, locations, and other such entities). Similar people are likely to be linked, and edges between these links indicate that linked users will influence each other and become more similar, two users in the same group or community if they have higher similarity.

Result visualization

Visualization helps one understand more about the data in hand. *A picture is worth a thousand words*. We get a better understanding of the feature space by representing data on a graphical platform. Trends, anomalies, relationships, and other similar patterns help us think more about the possible algorithm and heuristics to use on the given data for a given problem. There can be various levels of abstraction and granularities present in the data. Here's a list of a few standard methods used to visualize data:

- Boxplots
- Scatter plots
- Word clouds
- Decision trees
- Various social networks analysis tools such as Igraph, MuxViz, NetworkX, and so on

In the next chapters, we'll show you how these help us understand the results better. How to interpret the results is a crucial part of the mining process.

An example of social media mining

Let's look at a few examples of well-known social media sites:

Twitter

- What are people talking about right now?
- Mining entities from user's tweets
- Sentiment analysis

Facebook

- Gender analysis of Facebook post likes
- Analysis of Facebook friends network
- Inferring community behavior dynamically
- Fraud prevention
- Questions such as "Who influences whom?"
- Getting peoples' interest based on their chat history, such as with whom they are chatting, what they are chatting, where they are chatting, and so on.

Summary

In this chapter, we tried to familiarize the user with the concept of social media and mining.

We discussed the OAuth API, which offers a technique for clients to allow third-party entry to their resources without sharing their credentials. It also offers a way to grant controlled access in terms of scope and duration.

We saw examples of various R packages available to visualize the text data. We discussed innovative ways to analyze and study the text data via plots. The application of sentiment analysis along with topic mining was also discussed in the same sections. To many, it's a new way to look at these kinds of data. Historically, people have used plots to plot numerical data, but plotting words on 2D graphs is very new. People have made more advances than 2D plots. With Facebook and LinkedIn, the Gephi library allows visualizing the social networks in 3D.

Next, you learned the basic steps of any data-mining problem along with various machine learning algorithms. We'll see the applications of many of these algorithms in the coming chapters. We briefly talked about sentiment analysis, anomaly detection, and various community detection algorithms. So far, we have not gone deep into any of the algorithms, but will dive into them in the later chapters.

In the next chapter, we will apply the knowledge gained so far to mine Twitter and give detailed information of the methods and techniques used there.

2
Mining Opinions, Exploring Trends, and More with Twitter

Our approach in this book is to use statistics and social science theory to mine social media, and we'll use R as our base programming language.

In this chapter, we will cover the following:

- Twitter and its importance
- Getting hands-on with Twitter's data and using various Twitter APIs
- Use of data to solve business problems—comparison of various businesses based on tweets

Twitter and its importance

Twitter can be considered an extension of the short messages service, or SMS, but on an Internet-based platform. In the words of Jack Dorsey, co-founder and co-creator of Twitter:

> "...We came across the word 'twitter', and it was just perfect. The definition was 'a short burst of inconsequential information,' and 'chirps from birds'. And that's exactly what the product was."

Twitter acts as a utility with which people can send their *SMSs* to the whole world. It enables people to instantaneously get heard and get a response. Since the audience of this SMS is so large, responses are often very quick. Twitter facilitates the basic social instincts of humans. By sharing on Twitter, a user can easily express his/her opinion for just about everything, and at any time. Friends who are connected, or, in the case of Twitter, *followers*, immediately get the information about *what's going on in someone's life*. This in turn serves another human emotion—the innate need to know about what is going on in someone's life. Apart from being real-time, Twitter's UI is really easy to work with. It's naturally and instinctively understood. That is, the UI is very intuitive in nature.

Each tweet on Twitter is a short message with maximum of 140 characters. Twitter is an excellent example of a microblogging service. As of July 2014, the Twitter user base exceeded 500 million, with more than 271 million active users. Around 23 percent are adult Internet users, which is also about 19 percent of the entire adult population.

If we can properly mine what users are tweeting about, Twitter can act as a great tool for advertisement and marketing. However, this not the only information Twitter provides. Due to its non-symmetric nature in terms of followers and followings, Twitter assists better in terms of understanding user interests than for its impact on the social network. An interest graph can be thought of as a way to learn the links between individuals and their diverse interests. Computing the degree of association or correlations between individuals' interests and the potential advertisements is one of the most important applications of the interest graphs. Based on these correlations, a user can be targeted so as to attain a maximum response to an advertising campaign, along with followers' recommendations.

One interesting fact about Twitter (and Facebook) is that the user does not need to be a real person. A user on Twitter (or on Facebook) can be anything and anyone; for example, an organization, a campaign, or a famous but imaginary personality (a fictional character recognizable in the media) apart from a real/actual person. If a real person follows these users on Twitter, a lot can be inferred about their personality and hence ads or *other followers* can be recommended based on such information. For example, @fakingnews is an Indian blog that publishes news satires on subjects ranging from Indian politics to typical Indian mindsets. People who follow @fakingnews are ones who, in general, like to read sarcasm news. Hence, these people can be thought of as to belonging to the *same* cluster or community. If we have another sarcastic blog, we can always recommend it to this community and improve on advertisement return on investment. The chances of getting more hits via people belonging to this community will be higher than a community that doesn't follow @fakingnews, or any such news in general.

Once you have comprehended that Twitter allows you to create, link, and investigate a community with an interest in a random topic, the influence of Twitter and the knowledge one can find from mining it becomes clearer.

Understanding Twitter's APIs

Twitter APIs provide a means to access the Twitter data; that is, tweets sent by its millions of users. Let's get to know these APIs a bit better.

Twitter vocabulary

As described earlier, Twitter is a microblogging service with a social aspect. It allows its users to express their views/sentiments through an Internet SMS, called "tweets" in the context of Twitter. These tweets are entities formed of maximum of 140 characters. The content of these tweets can be anything ranging from a person's mood to person's location to a person's curiosity. The platform on which these tweets are posted is called a *Timeline*. To use Twitter's APIs, one must understand the basic terminology.

Tweets are the crux of Twitter. Theoretically, a tweet is just 140 characters of text content tweeted by a user, but there is more to it than just that. There is more metadata associated with the same tweet, which are classified by Twitter as entities and places:

- The entities consist of hashtags, URLs, and other media data that users have included in their tweets.
- The places are nothing but the locations from which the tweets originate. It is possible the place is the real world location from which the tweet was sent, or it could be a location mentioned in the text of the tweet.

Take the following tweet as an example:

Learn how to consume millions of tweets with @twitterapi at #TDC2014 in São Paulo #bigdata tomorrow at 2:10pm http://t.co/pTBlWzTvVd

The preceding tweet was tweeted by `@TwitterDev` and it's about 132 characters long. The following are the entities mentioned in this tweet:

- **Handle**: `@twitterapi`
- **Hashtags**: `#TDC2014`, `#bigdata`
- **URL**: `http://t.co/pTBlWzTvVd`

São Paulo is the place mentioned in this tweet.

This is an example of a tweet with a fairly good amount of metadata. Although the actual tweet's length is well within the 140-character limit, it contains more information than one can think of. This actually enables us to figure out that this tweet belongs to a specific community based on the cross-referencing of the topics present in the hashtags, the URL of the website, the different users mentioned, and so on. The interface (web or mobile) on which the tweets are displayed is called the **timeline**. The tweets are, in general, arranged in chronological order of posting time. On a specific user's account, only a certain number of tweets are displayed by Twitter. This is generally based on the users the given user is following and is being followed by. This is the interface a user will see when he/she login his/her Twitter account.

Twitter streams are different from a Twitter timeline in the sense that they are not for a specific user. The tweets on a user's Twitter timeline will be displayed from only a certain number of users, and will be displayed/updated less frequently, while the Twitter stream is a chronological collection of the all the tweets posted by all the users. The number of active users on Twitter is in the order of hundreds of millions. All the users tweeting during some public events of widespread interest, such as presidential debates, can achieve volumes of several hundreds of thousands of tweets per minute. The behavior is very similar to a stream; hence the name of such a collection is a Twitter stream.

You can try the following by creating a Twitter account (it would be more insightful if you have few followers already with you). Before creating the account, it is advised that you read all the terms and conditions of the site. You can also start reading its API documentation, but that is not mandatory for the step we will discuss in the next sections.

Creating a Twitter API connection

We need to have an app created at `https://dev.twitter.com/apps` before making any API requests to Twitter. It's a standard method for developers to gain API access, and, more importantly, it helps Twitter to observe and restricts developer from making high load API requests.

The `ROAuth` package is the one we are going to use in our experiments. Recall that in *Chapter 1, Fundamentals of Mining*, we discussed a lot about the `OAuth` protocol to for obtaining tokens. These tokens allow users to authorize third-party apps to access the data from any user account without the need to have their passwords (or other sensitive information). `ROAuth` basically facilitates the same thing.

Creating a new app

The first step toward getting any kind of token access from Twitter is to create an app on it. You have to go to `https://dev.twitter.com/` and log in with your Twitter credentials. Having logged in using your credentials, the step for creating an app are as follows:

1. Go to `https://apps.twitter.com/app/new`.

2. Put the name of your application in the **Name** field. This name can be anything you like.

3. Similarly, enter the description in the **Description** field.

4. The **Website** field needs to be filled with a valid URL, but, again, that can be any random URL.

5. You can leave the **Callback URL** field blank.

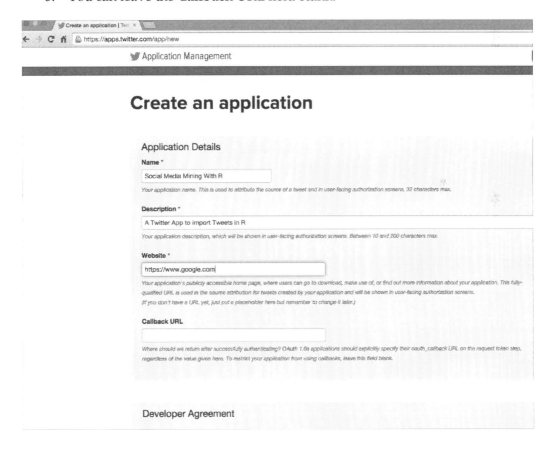

After the creation of this app, we need to find the **API Key** and **API Secret** values from the **Key and Access Token** tab. Consider the example shown in the following figure:

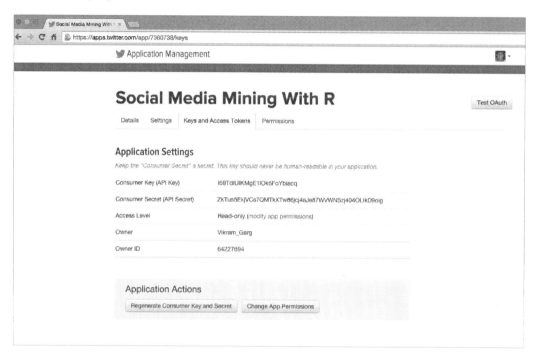

Under the **Key and Access Tokens** tab, you will find a button to generate access tokens. Click on it and you will be provided with an **Access Token** and **Access Token Secret** value.

Before using the preceding keys, we need to install `twitteR` to access the data in R using the app we just created. Use the following code:

```
install.packages(c("devtools", "rjson", "bit64", "httr"))
library(devtools)
install_github("geoffjentry/twitteR").
library(twitteR)
```

> **Downloading the example code**
>
> You can download the example code files from your account at
> http://www.packtpub.com for all the Packt Publishing books
> you have purchased. If you purchased this book elsewhere, you
> can visit http://www.packtpub.com/support and register to
> have the files e-mailed directly to you.

Here's sample code that helps us access the tweets posted since any given date and which contain a specific keyword. In this example, we are searching for tweets containing the word *Earthquake* in the tweets posted since *September 29, 2014*. In order to get this information, we provide four special types of information to get the authorization token:

- Key
- Secret
- Access token
- Access token secret

We'll show you how to use the preceding information to get an app authorized by the user and access its resources on Twitter. The ROAuh function in twitteR will make our next steps very smooth and clear:

```
api_key<- "your_api_key"
api_secret<- "your_api_secret"
access_token<- "your_access_token"
access_token_secret<- "your_access_token_secret"
setup_twitter_oauth
(api_key,api_secret,access_token,access_token_secret)
EarthQuakeTweets = searchTwitter("EarthQuake", since='2014-09-29')
```

You can also download the code from:
https://github.com/gargvikram07/SMMR_Twitter.

The results of this example should simply display **Using direct authentication** with 25 tweets loaded in the EarthQuakeTweets variable, as shown here.

```
head(EarthQuakeTweets,2)
[[1]]
[1] "TamamiJapan: RT @HistoricalPics: Japan. Top: One Month After
Hiroshima, 1945. Bottom: One Month After The Earthquake and Tsunami,
2011. Incredible. http…"

[[2]]
[1] "OldhamDs: RT @HistoricalPics: Japan. Top: One Month After
Hiroshima, 1945. Bottom: One Month After The Earthquake and Tsunami,
2011. Incredible. http…"
```

We have shown the first two of the 25 tweets containing the word *Earthquake* since September 29, 2014. If you closely observe the results, you'll find all the metadata we discussed in the previous section using str(EarthQuakeTweets[1]).

Finding trending topics

Now that you understand how to create API connections to Twitter and fetch data using it, we will look at how to get answer to *what is trending on Twitter* to list what topic (worldwide or local) is being talked about the most right now. Using the same API, we can easily access the trending information:

```
#return data frame with name, country & woeid.
Locs <- availableTrendLocations()
# Where woeid is a numerical identification code describing a location
ID

# Filter the data frame for Delhi (India) and extract the woeid of the
same
LocsIndia = subset(Locs, country == "India")
woeidDelhi = subset(LocsIndia, name == "Delhi")$woeid

# getTrends takes a specified woeid and returns the trending topics
associated with that woeid
trends = getTrends(woeid=woeidDelhi)
```

The function availableTrendLocations() returns R dataframe containing the name, country, and woeid parameters. We then filter this data frame for a location of our choosing; in this example, its *Delhi, India*. The function getTrends() fetches the top 10 trends in the location determined by the woeid.

Here are the top four trending hashtags in the region defined by woeid = 20070458, that is, *Delhi, India*:

```
head(trends)
name            url                       query              woeid
1 #AntiHinduNGOsExposed http://twitter.com/search?q=%23AntiHinduNGOsEx
posed %23AntiHinduNGOsExposed 20070458
2           #KhaasAadmi          http://twitter.com/search?q=%23Khaas
Aadmi           %23KhaasAadmi
20070458
3           #WinGOSF14          http://twitter.com/search?q=%23WinG
OSF14           %23WinGOSF14
20070458
4     #ItsForRealONeBay     http://twitter.com/search?q=%23ItsForReal
ONeBay
%23ItsForRealONeBay 20070458
```

Searching tweets

Similar to trends, there is one more important function that comes with the `TwitteR` package: `searchTwitter()`. This function will return tweets containing the searched string, along with the other constraints. Some of the constraints that can be imposed are as follows:

- `lang`: This constraints the tweets of given language
- `since`/`until`: This constraints the tweets to be *since* the given date or *until* the given date
- `geocode`: This constraints tweets to be from only those users who are located within a certain distance from the given latitude/longitude

For example, extracting tweets about the cricketer *Sachin Tendulkar* in the month of November 2014 returns the following:

```
head(searchTwitter('Sachin Tendulkar', since='2014-11-01',
until= '2014-11-30'))

[[1]]
[1] "TendulkarFC: RT @Moulinparikh: Sachin Tendulkar had a long
session with the Mumbai Ranji Trophy team after today's loss."

[[2]]
[1] "tyagi_niharika: @WahidRuba @Anuj_dvn @Neel_D_ @alishatariq3
@VWellwishers @Meenal_Rathore oh... Yaadaaya....hmaraesachuuu
sir\xed\xa0\xbd\xed\xb8\x8d..i mean sachin Tendulkar"

[[3]]
[1] "Meenal_Rathore: @WahidRuba @Anuj_dvn @tyagi_niharika @Neel_D_
@alishatariq3 @AliaaFcc @VWellwishers .. Sachin Tendulkar
\xed\xa0\xbd\xed\xb8\x8a☺"

[[4]]
[1] "MishraVidyanand: Vidyanand Mishra is following the Interest
\"The Living Legend SachinTendu...\" on http://t.co/tveHXMB4BM -
http://t.co/CocNMcxFge"

[[5]]
[1] "CSKalwaysWin: I have never tried to compare myself to anyone
else.\n - Sachin Tendulkar"
```

Twitter sentiment analysis

Depending on the objective, and based on the functionality to search any type of tweets from the public timeline, one can always collect the required corpus. For example, you may want to learn about customer satisfaction levels with various cab services, which are up and coming in the Indian market. These start-ups are offering various discounts and coupons to attract customers, but at the end of the day, the service quality determines the business of any organization. These start-ups are constantly promoting themselves on various social media websites. Customers are showing various sentiments on the same platform.

Let's target the following:

- **Meru Cabs**: A radio cabs service based in Mumbai, India, launched in 2007
- **Ola Cabs**: A taxi aggregator company based in Bangalore, India, launched in 2011
- **TaxiForSure**: A taxi aggregator company based in Bangalore, India, launched in 2011
- **Uber India**: A taxi aggregator company headquartered in San Francisco, California, launched in India in 2014

Let's make it our goal to get the general sentiments about each of the preceding service providers based on the customer sentiments present in the tweets on Twitter.

Collecting tweets as a corpus

We'll start with the `searchTwitter()` function (discussed previously) on the `TwitteR` package to gather the tweets for each of the preceding organizations.

Now, in order to avoid writing the same code again and again, we push the following authorization code in the file called `authenticate.R`:

```
library(twitteR)
api_key<- "xx"
api_secret<- "xx"
access_token<- "xx"
access_token_secret<- "xx"
setup_twitter_oauth(api_key,api_secret,access_token,
access_token_secret)
```

We run the following scripts to get the required tweets:

```
# Load the necessary packages
source('authenticate.R')

Meru_tweets = searchTwitter("MeruCabs", n=2000, lang="en")
Ola_tweets = searchTwitter("OlaCabs", n=2000, lang="en")
TaxiForSure_tweets =
searchTwitter("TaxiForSure", n=2000, lang="en")
Uber_tweets = searchTwitter("Uber_Delhi", n=2000, lang="en")
```

Now, as mentioned in Twitter's Rest API documentation, we get the message **"Due to capacity constraints, the index currently only covers about a week's worth of tweets"**. We do not always get the desired number of tweets (for example, here, it's 2,000). Instead, the following are the sizes of each of the preceding tweet lists we get the following:

```
>length(Meru_tweets)
[1]  393
>length(Ola_tweets)
[1]  984
> length(TaxiForSure_tweets)
[1]  720
> length(Uber_tweets)
[1]  2000
```

As you can see from the preceding code, the length of these tweets is not equal to the number of tweets we asked for in our query scripts. There are many things to take away from this information. Since these tweets are only from the last week's tweets on Twitter, they suggest there is more discussion about these taxi services in the following order:

- Uber India
- Ola Cabs
- TaxiForSure
- Meru Cabs

A ban was imposed on Uber India after an alleged rape incident by one Uber India driver. The decision to put a ban on the entire organization because one of its drivers committed a crime became a matter of public outrage. Hence, the number of tweets about Uber increased on social media. Now, Meru Cabs have been in India for almost seven years. Hence, they are quite a stable organization. The amount of promotion Ola Cabs and TaxiForSure are doing is way higher than that done by Meru Cabs. This could be one reason for Meru Cabs having the lowest number (393) of tweets in last week. The number of tweets in the last week is comparable for Ola Cabs (984) and TaxiForSure (720). There could be several reasons for this. They both started their business in same year, and, more importantly, they follow the same business model. Meru Cabs is a radio taxi service and they own and manage a fleet of cars, while Ola Cabs, TaxiForSure, or Uber are a marketplace for users to compare the offerings of various operators and book easily.

Let's dive deep into the data and get more insights.

Cleaning the corpus

Before applying any intelligent algorithms to gather more insights from the tweets collected so far, let's first clean the corpus. In order to clean up, we need to understand what the list of tweets looks like:

```
head(Meru_tweets)
[[1]]
[1] "MeruCares: @KapilTwitts 2&gt;...and other details at
feedback@merucabs.com We'll check back and reach out soon."

[[2]]
[1] "vikasraidhan: @MeruCabs really disappointed with @GenieCabs.
Cab is never assigned on time. Driver calls after 30 minutes. Why
would I ride with Meru?"

[[3]]
[1] "shiprachowdhary: fallback of #ubershame , #MERUCABS taking
customers for a ride"

[[4]]
[1] "shiprachowdhary: They book Genie, but JIT inform of
cancellation &amp; send full fare #MERUCABS . Very
disappointed.Always used these guys 4 and recommend them."

[[5]]
[1] "shiprachowdhary: No choice bt to take the #merucabs premium
service. Driver told me that this happens a lot with #merucabs."
```

```
[[6]]
[1] "shiprachowdhary: booked #Merucabsyestrdy. Asked for Meru
Genie. 10 mins 4 pick up time, they call to say Genie not available,
so sending the full fare cab"
```

The first tweet here is a grievance solution, while the second, fourth, and fifth are actually customer sentiments about the services provided by Meru Cabs. We see the following:

- Lots of meta information such as @people, URLs and #hashtags
- Punctuation marks, numbers, and unnecessary spaces
- Some of these tweets are retweets from other users; for the given application, we would not like to consider **retweets (RTs)** in sentiment analysis

We clean all these data by using the following code block:

```
MeruTweets <- sapply(Meru_tweets, function(x) x$getText())
OlaTweets = sapply(Ola_tweets, function(x) x$getText())
TaxiForSureTweets = sapply(TaxiForSure_tweets,
function(x) x$getText())
UberTweets = sapply(Uber_tweets, function(x) x$getText())

catch.error = function(x)
{
  # let us create a missing value for test purpose
  y = NA
  # Try to catch that error (NA) we just created
catch_error = tryCatch(tolower(x), error=function(e) e)
  # if not an error
  if (!inherits(catch_error, "error"))
    y = tolower(x)
  # check result if error exists, otherwise the function works fine.
  return(y)
}

cleanTweets<- function(tweet){
  # Clean the tweet for sentiment analysis
  #  remove html links, which are not required for sentiment analysis
tweet = gsub("(f|ht)(tp)(s?)(://)(.*)[.|/](.*)", " ", tweet)
  # First we will remove retweet entities from
the stored tweets (text)
  tweet = gsub("(RT|via)((?:\\b\\W*@\\w+)+)", " ", tweet)
  # Then remove all "#Hashtag"
  tweet = gsub("#\\w+", " ", tweet)
  # Then remove all "@people"
```

```
  tweet = gsub("@\\w+", " ", tweet)
  # Then remove all the punctuation
  tweet = gsub("[[:punct:]]", " ", tweet)
 # Then remove numbers, we need only text for analytics
 tweet = gsub("[[:digit:]]", " ", tweet)
  # finally, we remove unnecessary spaces (white spaces, tabs etc)
  tweet = gsub("[ \t]{2,}", " ", tweet)
  tweet = gsub("^\\s+|\\s+$", "", tweet)
  # if anything else, you feel, should be removed, you can.
For example "slang words" etc using the above function and methods.
  # Next we'll convert all the word in lower case.
This makes uniform pattern.
  tweet = catch.error(tweet)
  tweet
}


cleanTweetsAndRemoveNAs<- function(Tweets) {
TweetsCleaned = sapply(Tweets, cleanTweets)
# Remove the "NA" tweets from this tweet list
TweetsCleaned = TweetsCleaned[!is.na(TweetsCleaned)]
  names(TweetsCleaned) = NULL
# Remove the repetitive tweets from this tweet list
TweetsCleaned = unique(TweetsCleaned)
TweetsCleaned
}


MeruTweetsCleaned = cleanTweetsAndRemoveNAs(MeruTweets)
OlaTweetsCleaned = cleanTweetsAndRemoveNAs(OlaTweets)
TaxiForSureTweetsCleaned <-
cleanTweetsAndRemoveNAs(TaxiForSureTweets)
UberTweetsCleaned = cleanTweetsAndRemoveNAs(UberTweets)
```

Here's the size of each of the cleaned tweet lists:

```
> length(MeruTweetsCleaned)
[1] 309
> length(OlaTweetsCleaned)
[1] 811
> length(TaxiForSureTweetsCleaned)
[1] 574
> length(UberTweetsCleaned)
[1] 1355
```

Estimating sentiment (A)

There are many sophisticated resources available for estimating sentiments. Many research papers and software packages are available open source, and they implement very complex algorithms for sentiment analysis. After getting the cleaned Twitter data, we are going to use few such R packages to assess the sentiments in the tweets.

It's worth mentioning here that not all the tweets represent sentiments. A few tweets can be just information/facts, while others can be customer care responses. Ideally, they should not be used to assess the customer sentiment about a particular organization.

As a first step, we'll use a Naïve algorithm, which gives a score based on the number of times a positive or a negative word occurred in the given sentence (and, in our case, in a tweet).

Please download the positive and negative opinion/sentiment (nearly 68,000) words from English language. This *opinion lexicon* will be used as a first example in our sentiment analysis experiment. The good thing about this approach is that we are relying on highly researched, and at the same time customizable, input parameters. Here are a few examples of existing positive and negative sentiment words:

- **Positive**: Love, best, cool, great, good, and amazing
- **Negative**: Hate, worst, sucks, awful, and nightmare

```
>opinion.lexicon.pos =
scan('opinion-lexicon-English/positive-words.txt',
what='character', comment.char=';')
>opinion.lexicon.neg =
scan('opinion-lexicon-English/negative-words.txt',
what='character', comment.char=';')
> head(opinion.lexicon.neg)
[1] "2-faced"     "2-faces"      "abnormal"    "abolish"
"abominable" "abominably"
> head(opinion.lexicon.pos)
[1] "a+"          "abound"       "abounds"     "abundance"  "abundant"
"accessable"
```

We'll add a few industry-specific and/or especially emphatic terms based on our requirements:

```
pos.words = c(opinion.lexicon.pos,'upgrade')
neg.words = c(opinion.lexicon.neg,'wait',
'waiting', 'wtf', 'cancellation')
```

Now, we create a function, `score.sentiment()`, which computes the raw sentiment based on the simple matching algorithm:

```
getSentimentScore = function(sentences, words.positive,
words.negative, .progress='none')
{
  require(plyr)
  require(stringr)

  scores = laply(sentences,
function(sentence, words.positive, words.negative) {

    # Let first remove the Digit, Punctuation character and Control
characters:
    sentence = gsub('[[:cntrl:]]', '', gsub('[[:punct:]]', '',
gsub('\\d+', '', sentence)))

    # Then lets convert all to lower sentence case:
    sentence = tolower(sentence)

    # Now lets split each sentence by the space delimiter
    words = unlist(str_split(sentence, '\\s+'))

    # Get the boolean match of each words with the positive & negative
opinion-lexicon
    pos.matches = !is.na(match(words, words.positive))
    neg.matches = !is.na(match(words, words.negative))

    # Now get the score as total positive sentiment minus the total
negatives
    score = sum(pos.matches) - sum(neg.matches)

    return(score)
  }, words.positive, words.negative, .progress=.progress )

  # Return a data frame with respective sentence and the score
  return(data.frame(text=sentences, score=scores))
}
```

Now, we apply the preceding function to the corpus of tweets collected and cleaned so far:

```
MeruResult = getSentimentScore(MeruTweetsCleaned, words.positive ,
words.negative)
OlaResult = getSentimentScore(OlaTweetsCleaned, words.positive ,
words.negative)
TaxiForSureResult = getSentimentScore(TaxiForSureTweetsCleaned,
words.positive , words.negative) UberResult =
getSentimentScore(UberTweetsCleaned, words.positive ,
words.negative)
```

Here are some sample results:

Tweet for Meru Cabs	Score
gt and other details at feedback com we ll check back and reach out soon	0
really disappointed with cab is never assigned on time driver calls after minutes why would i ride with meru	-1
so after years of bashing today i m pleasantly surprised clean car courteous driver prompt pickup mins efficient route	4
a min drive cost hrs used to cost less ur unreliable and expensive trying to lose ur customers	-3
Tweet For Ola Cabs	**Score**
the service is going from bad to worse the drivers deny to come after a confirmed booking	-3
love the olacabs app give it a swirl sign up with my referral code dxf n and earn rs download the app from	1
crn kept me waiting for mins amp at last moment driver refused pickup so unreliable amp irresponsible	-4
this is not the first time has delighted me punctuality and free upgrade awesome that	4
Tweet For TaxiForSure	**Score**
great service now i have become a regular customer of tfs thank you for the upgrade as well happy taxi ing saving	5
really disappointed with cab is never assigned on time driver calls after minutes why would i ride with meru	-1
horrible taxi service had to wait for one hour with a new born in the chilly weather of new delhi waiting for them	-4
what do i get now if you resolve the issue after i lost a crucial business because of the taxi delay	-3

Tweet For Uber India	Score
that s good uber s fares will prob be competitive til they gain local monopoly then will go sky high as in new york amp delhi saving	3
from a shabby backend app stack to daily pr fuck ups its increasingly obvious that is run by child minded blow hards	-3
you say that uber is illegally running were you stupid to not ban earlier and only ban it now after the rape	-3
perhaps uber biz model does need some looking into it s not just in delhi that this happens but in boston too	0

From the preceding observations, it's clear that this basic sentiment analysis method works fine in normal circumstances, but in the case of Uber India, the results deviated too much from a subjective score. It's safe to say that basic word-matching gives a good indicator of overall customer sentiment, except in cases where the data itself is not reliable. In our case, the tweets from Uber India are not really related to the services that Uber provides, but rather the one incident of crime by its driver, which made the whole score go haywire:

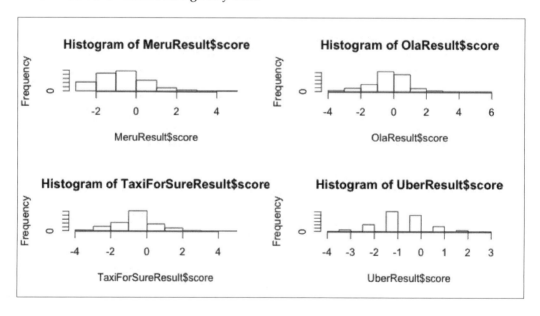

Let's not compute a point statistic for the scores we have computed so far. Since the numbers of tweets are not equal for each of the four organizations, we compute a mean and standard deviation for each.

Organization	Mean Sentiment Score	Standard Deviation
Meru Cabs	-0.2218543	1.301846
Ola Cabs	0.197724	1.170334
TaxiForSure	-0.09841828	1.154056
Uber India	-0.6132666	1.071094

Estimating sentiment (B)

Let's now move one step further. Instead of using simple matching of opinion lexicon, we'll use something called *Naive Bayes* to decide on the emotion present in any tweet. We will require packages called `Rstem` and `sentiment` to assist with this. It's important to mention here that both these packages are no longer available in CRAN, so we have to provide the repository location as a parameter `install.package()` function. Here's the R script to install the required packages:

```
install.packages("Rstem",
repos = "http://www.omegahat.org/R", type="source")
require(devtools)
install_url("http://cran.r-project.org/src/contrib/Archive/sentiment/
sentiment_0.2.tar.gz") require(sentiment)
ls("package:sentiment")
```

Now that we have the `sentiment` and `Rstem` packages installed in our R workspace, we can build the `bayes` classifier for sentiment analysis:

```
library(sentiment)
# classify_emotion function returns an object of class data frame #
with seven columns (anger, disgust, fear, joy, sadness, surprise,  #
# best_fit) and one row for each document:
MeruTweetsClassEmo = classify_emotion(MeruTweetsCleaned,
algorithm="bayes", prior=1.0)
OlaTweetsClassEmo = classify_emotion(OlaTweetsCleaned,
algorithm="bayes", prior=1.0)
TaxiForSureTweetsClassEmo =
classify_emotion(TaxiForSureTweetsCleaned, algorithm="bayes",
prior=1.0)
UberTweetsClassEmo = classify_emotion(UberTweetsCleaned,
algorithm="bayes", prior=1.0)
```

The following figure shows a few results from Bayesian analysis using the `sentiment` package for Meru Cabs tweets. Similarly, we generated results for other cab services from our problem setup.

The `sentiment` package was built to use a *trained* dataset of emotion words (nearly 1,500 words). The function `classify_emotion()` generates results belonging to one of the following six emotions: **anger**, **disgust**, **fear**, **joy**, **sadness**, and **surprise**. When the system is not able to classify the overall emotion as any of the six, NA is returned:

```
> head(MeruTweetsClassEmo,20)
        ANGER               DISGUST             FEAR                JOY                 SADNESS             SURPRISE            BEST_FIT
 [1,]  "1.46871776464786"  "3.09234031207392"  "2.06783599555953"  "1.02547755260094"  "1.7277074477352"   "2.78695866252273"  NA
 [2,]  "1.46871776464786"  "3.09234031207392"  "2.06783599555953"  "1.02547755260094"  "1.7277074477352"   "2.78695866252273"  NA
 [3,]  "1.46871776464786"  "3.09234031207392"  "2.06783599555953"  "1.02547755260094"  "1.7277074477352"   "2.78695866252273"  NA
 [4,]  "1.46871776464786"  "3.09234031207392"  "2.06783599555953"  "1.02547755260094"  "1.7277074477352"   "2.78695866252273"  NA
 [5,]  "1.46871776464786"  "3.09234031207392"  "2.06783599555953"  "1.02547755260094"  "1.7277074477352"   "2.78695866252273"  NA
 [6,]  "1.46871776464786"  "3.09234031207392"  "2.06783599555953"  "7.34083555412328"  "1.7277074477352"   "2.78695866252273"  "joy"
 [7,]  "1.46871776464786"  "3.09234031207392"  "2.06783599555953"  "1.02547755260094"  "1.7277074477352"   "2.78695866252273"  NA
 [8,]  "1.46871776464786"  "3.09234031207392"  "2.06783599555953"  "13.6561935556456"  "1.7277074477352"   "7.34083555412327"  "joy"
 [9,]  "1.46871776464786"  "3.09234031207392"  "2.06783599555953"  "1.02547755260094"  "1.7277074477352"   "2.78695866252273"  NA
[10,]  "1.46871776464786"  "3.09234031207392"  "2.06783599555953"  "7.34083555412328"  "1.7277074477352"   "2.78695866252273"  "joy"
[11,]  "1.46871776464786"  "3.09234031207392"  "2.06783599555953"  "7.34083555412328"  "1.7277074477352"   "2.78695866252273"  "joy"
[12,]  "1.46871776464786"  "3.09234031207392"  "2.06783599555953"  "1.02547755260094"  "7.34083555412328"  "2.78695866252273"  "sadness"
[13,]  "1.46871776464786"  "3.09234031207392"  "2.06783599555953"  "1.02547755260094"  "1.7277074477352"   "2.78695866252273"  NA
[14,]  "1.46871776464786"  "3.09234031207392"  "2.06783599555953"  "1.02547755260094"  "7.34083555412328"  "7.34083555412327"  "sadness"
[15,]  "1.46871776464786"  "3.09234031207392"  "2.06783599555953"  "1.02547755260094"  "1.7277074477352"   "2.78695866252273"  NA
[16,]  "1.46871776464786"  "3.09234031207392"  "2.06783599555953"  "7.34083555412328"  "7.34083555412328"  "2.78695866252273"  "joy"
[17,]  "7.34083555412328"  "3.09234031207392"  "2.06783599555953"  "1.02547755260094"  "1.7277074477352"   "2.78695866252273"  "anger"
[18,]  "7.34083555412328"  "3.09234031207392"  "2.06783599555953"  "1.02547755260094"  "1.7277074477352"   "2.78695866252273"  "anger"
[19,]  "1.46871776464786"  "3.09234031207392"  "2.06783599555953"  "13.6561935556456"  "1.7277074477352"   "2.78695866252273"  "joy"
[20,]  "1.46871776464786"  "3.09234031207392"  "2.06783599555953"  "1.02547755260094"  "1.7277074477352"   "2.78695866252273"  NA
```

Let's substitute these NA values with the word unknown to make further analysis easier:

```
# we will fetch emotion category best_fit for our analysis purposes.
MeruEmotion = MeruTweetsClassEmo[,7]
OlaEmotion = OlaTweetsClassEmo[,7]
TaxiForSureEmotion = TaxiForSureTweetsClassEmo[,7]
UberEmotion = UberTweetsClassEmo[,7]

MeruEmotion[is.na(MeruEmotion)] = "unknown"
OlaEmotion[is.na(OlaEmotion)] = "unknown"
TaxiForSureEmotion[is.na(TaxiForSureEmotion)] = "unknown"
UberEmotion[is.na(UberEmotion)] = "unknown"
```

The best-fit emotions present in these tweets are as follows:

```
> head(MeruEmotion,20)       > head(OlaEmotion,20)          > head(TaxiForSureEmotion,20)      > head(UberEmotion,20)
 [1] NA       NA              [1] NA       NA                 [1] NA       NA                     [1] NA       NA
 [3] NA       NA              [3] "sadness" "sadness"         [3] "sadness" "sadness"             [3] NA       "anger"
 [5] NA       "joy"           [5] "sadness" "joy"             [5] "sadness" "sadness"             [5] NA       NA
 [7] NA       "joy"           [7] NA       NA                 [7] NA       NA                     [7] NA       NA
 [9] NA       "joy"           [9] NA       NA                 [9] "joy"    NA                     [9] NA       NA
[11] "joy"    "sadness"      [11] NA       "joy"             [11] NA       NA                    [11] NA       "sadness"
[13] NA       "sadness"      [13] "fear"   "joy"             [13] NA       NA                    [13] NA       NA
[15] NA       "joy"          [15] "surprise" "joy"           [15] "sadness" NA                   [15] NA       NA
[17] "anger"  "anger"        [17] NA       "joy"             [17] NA       "joy"                 [17] NA       NA
[19] "joy"    NA             [19] "joy"    NA                [19] NA       NA                    [19] NA       NA
```

Further, we'll use another function, `classify_polarity()`, provided by the `sentiment` package, to classify the tweets into two classes, `pos` (positive sentiment) and `neg` (negative sentiment). The idea is to compute the log likelihood of a tweet, assuming it belongs to either of the two classes. Once these likelihoods are calculated, a ratio of the pos-likelihood to neg-likelihood is calculated, and, based on this ratio, the tweets are classified as belonging to a particular class. It's important to note that if this ratio turns out to be 1, then the overall sentiment of the tweet is assumed to be "neutral". The code is as follows:

```
MeruTweetsClassPol = classify_polarity(MeruTweetsCleaned,
algorithm="bayes")
OlaTweetsClassPol = classify_polarity(OlaTweetsCleaned,
algorithm="bayes")
TaxiForSureTweetsClassPol =
classify_polarity(TaxiForSureTweetsCleaned, algorithm="bayes")
UberTweetsClassPol = classify_polarity(UberTweetsCleaned,
algorithm="bayes")
```

We get the following output:

```
> head(MeruTweetsClassPol,20)
        POS                  NEG                   POS/NEG                 BEST_FIT
 [1,]  "8.78232285939751"   "0.445453222112551"   "19.7154772340574"      "positive"
 [2,]  "1.03127774142571"   "9.47547003995745"    "0.108836578774127"     "negative"
 [3,]  "1.03127774142571"   "0.445453222112551"   "2.31512017476245"      "positive"
 [4,]  "17.2265151579293"   "18.5054868578024"    "0.930886892644283"     "negative"
 [5,]  "8.78232285939751"   "0.445453222112551"   "19.7154772340574"      "positive"
 [6,]  "1.03127774142571"   "18.5054868578024"    "0.0557282145209216"    "negative"
 [7,]  "9.47547003995745"   "0.445453222112551"   "21.2715265477714"      "positive"
 [8,]  "49.6169899909363"   "0.445453222112551"   "111.385410471674"      "positive"
 [9,]  "1.03127774142571"   "0.445453222112551"   "2.31512017476245"      "positive"
[10,]  "17.2265151579293"   "9.47547003995745"    "1.81801167491282"      "neutral"
[11,]  "17.2265151579293"   "9.47547003995745"    "1.81801167491282"      "neutral"
[12,]  "8.78232285939751"   "9.47547003995745"    "0.926848253686942"     "negative"
[13,]  "25.670707456461"    "9.47547003995745"    "2.70917509613869"      "positive"
[14,]  "16.5333679773693"   "17.8123396772424"    "0.928197433742679"     "negative"
[15,]  "17.9196623384892"   "0.445453222112551"   "40.2279329207804"      "positive"
[16,]  "8.78232285939751"   "9.47547003995745"    "0.926848253686942"     "negative"
[17,]  "8.78232285939751"   "9.47547003995745"    "0.926848253686942"     "negative"
[18,]  "17.2265151579293"   "0.445453222112551"   "38.6718836070664"      "positive"
[19,]  "1.03127774142571"   "9.47547003995745"    "0.108836578774127"     "negative"
[20,]  "8.78232285939751"   "8.78232285939751"    "1"                     "neutral"
```

The preceding figure shows a few results obtained by using the `classify_polarity()` function of the `sentiment` package for Meru Cabs tweets. We'll now generate consolidated results from the two functions in a data frame for each cab service for plotting purposes:

```
# we will fetch polarity category best_fit for our analysis purposes,
MeruPol = MeruTweetsClassPol[,4]
OlaPol = OlaTweetsClassPol[,4]
TaxiForSurePol = TaxiForSureTweetsClassPol[,4]
UberPol = UberTweetsClassPol[,4]


# Let us now create a data frame with the above results
MeruSentimentDataFrame = data.frame(text=MeruTweetsCleaned,
emotion=MeruEmotion, polarity=MeruPol, stringsAsFactors=FALSE)
OlaSentimentDataFrame = data.frame(text=OlaTweetsCleaned,
emotion=OlaEmotion, polarity=OlaPol, stringsAsFactors=FALSE)
```

```
TaxiForSureSentimentDataFrame =
data.frame(text=TaxiForSureTweetsCleaned,
emotion=TaxiForSureEmotion, polarity=TaxiForSurePol,
stringsAsFactors=FALSE)
UberSentimentDataFrame = data.frame(text=UberTweetsCleaned,
emotion=UberEmotion, polarity=UberPol, stringsAsFactors=FALSE)


# rearrange data inside the frame by sorting it
MeruSentimentDataFrame = within(MeruSentimentDataFrame, emotion <-
factor(emotion, levels=names(sort(table(emotion),
decreasing=TRUE))))
OlaSentimentDataFrame = within(OlaSentimentDataFrame, emotion <-
factor(emotion, levels=names(sort(table(emotion),
decreasing=TRUE))))
TaxiForSureSentimentDataFrame =
within(TaxiForSureSentimentDataFrame, emotion <- factor(emotion,
levels=names(sort(table(emotion), decreasing=TRUE))))
UberSentimentDataFrame = within(UberSentimentDataFrame, emotion <-
factor(emotion, levels=names(sort(table(emotion),
decreasing=TRUE))))
plotSentiments1<- function (sentiment_dataframe,title) {
  library(ggplot2)
ggplot(sentiment_dataframe, aes(x=emotion)) +
geom_bar(aes(y=..count.., fill=emotion)) +
scale_fill_brewer(palette="Dark2") +
ggtitle(title) +
    theme(legend.position='right') + ylab('Number of Tweets') +
xlab('Emotion Categories')
}


plotSentiments1(MeruSentimentDataFrame, 'Sentiment Analysis of
Tweets on Twitter about MeruCabs')
plotSentiments1(OlaSentimentDataFrame, 'Sentiment Analysis of
Tweets on Twitter about OlaCabs')
plotSentiments1(TaxiForSureSentimentDataFrame, 'Sentiment Analysis
of Tweets on Twitter about TaxiForSure')
plotSentiments1(UberSentimentDataFrame, 'Sentiment Analysis of
Tweets on Twitter about UberIndia')
```

The output is as follows:

```
> head(MeruSentimentDataFrame,20)
                                                                                          text emotion polarity
1                        gt and other details at feedback com we ll check back and reach out soon    <NA> positive
2                  really disappointed with cab is never assigned on time driver calls after minutes why would i ride with meru    <NA> negative
3                                                              fallback of taking customers for a ride    <NA> positive
4   they book genie but jit inform of cancellation amp send full fare very disappointed always used these guys and recommend them    <NA> negative
5                                         no choice bt to take the premium service driver told me that this happens a lot with    <NA> positive
6    booked yestrdy asked for meru genie mins pick up time they call to say genie not available so sending the full fare cab     joy negative
7                        the ad is just fab but what s the use if the app is buggy i have a mbps connection up and running    <NA> positive
8                           effortless cab journeys with a great experience book through the amp enjoy amazing benefits     joy positive
9                               can anyone give me a cab tomorrow pm from kadugodi to kr puram bangalore anyone    <NA> positive
10                   good afternoon and welcome to chennai do check out a new way of traveling in the city with meru cabs     joy  neutral
11                      good afternoon and welcome to pune do check out a new way of traveling in the city with meru cabs     joy  neutral
12            hi we re sorry that this happened to help trace your booking plz share booking id or mobile no at feedback sadness negative
13   when you re in mumbai do experience the brand new meru cab journey to make road travel more effortless than ever before    <NA> positive
14                    catching up with family and friends this winter use a meru and get cash back on payments through sadness negative
15               nt gng to recommend meru to any one atleast learn from they have the courtesy to infm cust regd any issues    <NA> positive
16    due to this got late for imp meeting tdy had really bad experience with meru change your slogan to don t rely on us     joy negative
17              is there an email address i can mail my grievance mails feedback com bounce back as mailbox is full   anger negative
```

In the preceding figure, we showed sample results generated on Meru Cabs tweets using both the functions. Let's now plot them one by one. First, let's create a single function to be used by each business's tweets. We call it `plotSentiments1()` and then we plot it for each business:

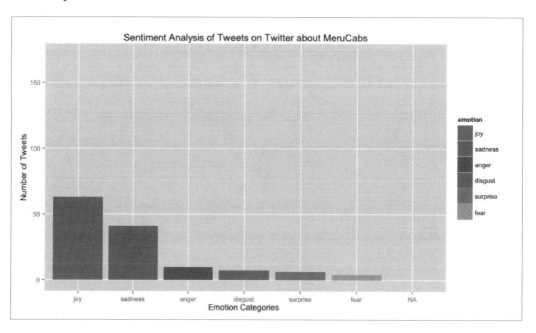

The following dashboard shows the analysis for Ola Cabs:

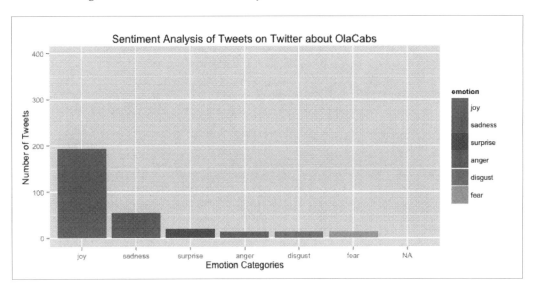

The following dashboard shows the analysis for TaxiForSure:

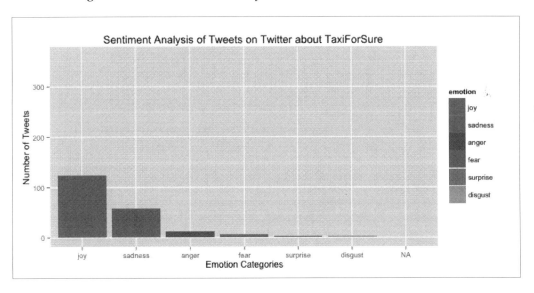

The following dashboard shows the analysis for Uber India:

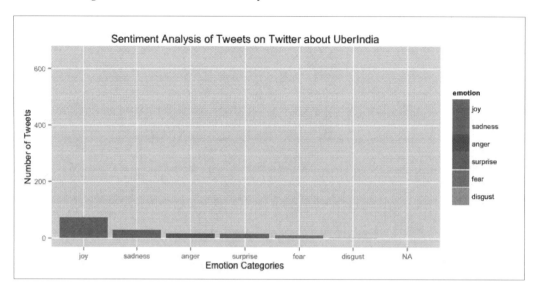

These sentiments basically reflect observations broadly similar to those we made with the basic word-matching algorithm. The number of tweets with **joy** constitute the largest part of tweets for all these organizations, indicating that these organizations are trying their best to provide good business in the country. The **sadness** tweets are less numerous than the **joy** tweets. However, if compared with each other, they indicate the overall market share versus the level of customer satisfaction with each service provider. Similarly, these graphs can be used to assess the level of dissatisfaction in terms of **anger** and **disgust** in the tweets. Let's now consider only the positive and negative sentiments present in the tweets:

```
# Similarly we will plot distribution of polarity in the tweets
plotSentiments2 <- function (sentiment_dataframe,title) {
  library(ggplot2)
ggplot(sentiment_dataframe, aes(x=polarity)) +
geom_bar(aes(y=..count.., fill=polarity)) +
scale_fill_brewer(palette="RdGy") +
ggtitle(title) +
    theme(legend.position='right') + ylab('Number of Tweets') +
xlab('Polarity Categories')
}

plotSentiments2(MeruSentimentDataFrame, 'Polarity Analysis of
Tweets on Twitter about MeruCabs')
plotSentiments2(OlaSentimentDataFrame, 'Polarity Analysis of
Tweets on Twitter about OlaCabs')
```

```
plotSentiments2(TaxiForSureSentimentDataFrame, 'Polarity Analysis
of Tweets on Twitter about TaxiForSure')
plotSentiments2(UberSentimentDataFrame, 'Polarity Analysis of
Tweets on Twitter about UberIndia')
```

The output is as follows:

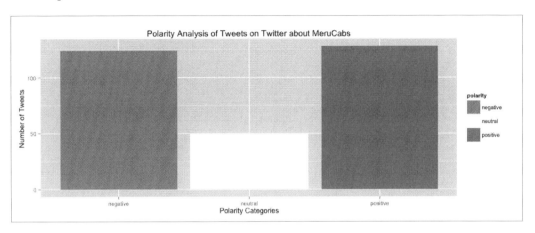

The following dashboard shows the polarity analysis for Ola Cabs:

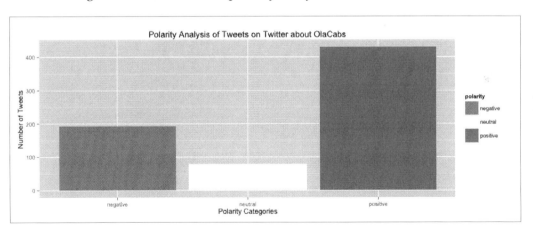

The following dashboard shows the analysis for TaxiForSure:

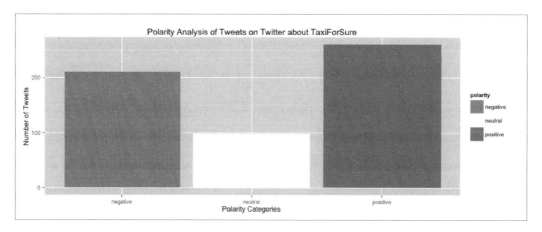

The following dashboard shows the analysis for Uber India:

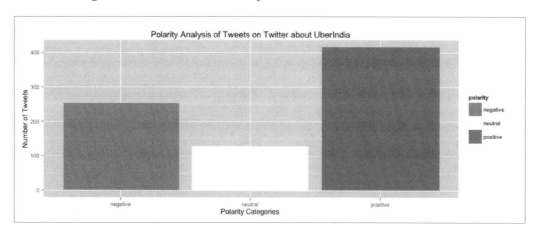

It's a basic human trait to inform others about what's wrong rather than informing them if there was something right. We tend to tweet/report if something bad happens rather reporting/tweeting if an experience was rather good. Hence, the negative tweets are expected to be larger than the positive tweets in general. Still, over a period of time (a week in our case), the ratio of the two easily reflects the overall market share versus the level of customer satisfaction for each service provider. Next, we try to get a sense of the overall content of the tweets by using the word clouds discussed in *Chapter 1, Fundamentals of Mining*.

```
removeCustomeWords <- function (TweetsCleaned) {
  for(i in 1:length(TweetsCleaned)){
    TweetsCleaned[i] <- tryCatch({
      TweetsCleaned[i] =  removeWords(TweetsCleaned[i],
c(stopwords("english"), "care", "guys", "can", "dis", "didn",
"guy" ,"booked", "plz"))
      TweetsCleaned[i]
    }, error=function(cond) {
      TweetsCleaned[i]
    }, warning=function(cond) {
      TweetsCleaned[i]
    })
  }
  return(TweetsCleaned)
}


getWordCloud <- function
(sentiment_dataframe, TweetsCleaned, Emotion) {
  emos = levels(factor(sentiment_dataframe$emotion))
  n_emos = length(emos)
  emo.docs = rep("", n_emos)
  TweetsCleaned = removeCustomeWords(TweetsCleaned)

  for (i in 1:n_emos){
    emo.docs[i] = paste(TweetsCleaned[Emotion ==
emos[i]], collapse=" ")
  }
  corpus = Corpus(VectorSource(emo.docs))
  tdm = TermDocumentMatrix(corpus)
  tdm = as.matrix(tdm)
  colnames(tdm) = emos
  require(wordcloud)
  suppressWarnings(comparison.cloud(tdm, colors =
brewer.pal(n_emos, "Dark2"),  scale = c(3,.5), random.order =
FALSE, title.size = 1.5))
}
getWordCloud(MeruSentimentDataFrame, MeruTweetsCleaned,
MeruEmotion)
```

```
getWordCloud(OlaSentimentDataFrame, OlaTweetsCleaned, OlaEmotion)
getWordCloud(TaxiForSureSentimentDataFrame, TaxiForSureTweetsCleaned,
TaxiForSureEmotion)
getWordCloud(UberSentimentDataFrame, UberTweetsCleaned, UberEmotion)
```

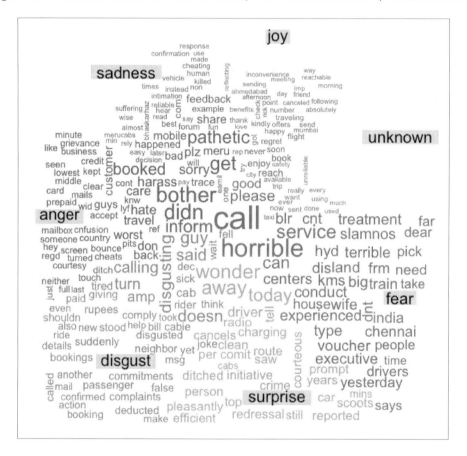

The preceding figure shows the word cloud from tweets about Meru Cabs.

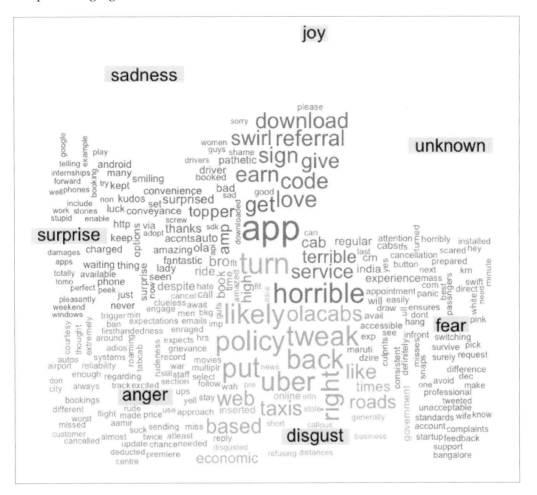

The preceding figure shows the word cloud from tweets about Ola Cabs.

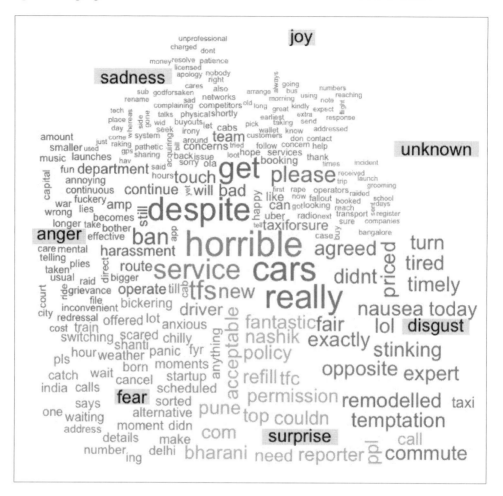

The preceding figure shows the word cloud from tweets about TaxiForSure.

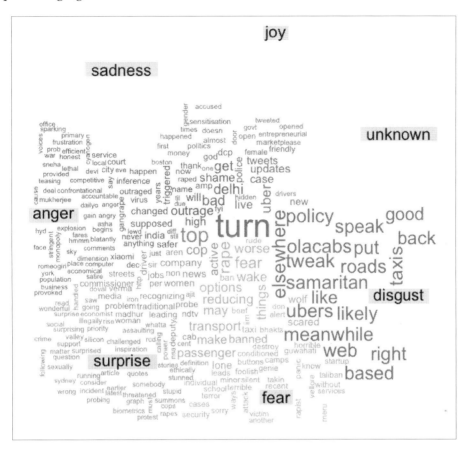

The preceding figure shows word cloud from tweets about Uber India.

Summary

In this chapter, you gained knowledge of the various Twitter APIs. We discussed how to create a connection with Twitter, and we saw how to retrieve tweets with various attributes. We saw the power of Twitter in helping us determine customers' attitudes toward today's various businesses. The activity can be done on a weekly basis, and one easily get the monthly, quarterly, or yearly changes in customer sentiment. This can not only help the customer decide the trending business, but also the business itself can get a well-defined metric of its own performance. It can use such scores/graphs to improve. We also discussed various methods of sentiment analysis, varying from basic word-matching the advanced Bayesian algorithms.

In the next chapter, we will apply a similar analysis to Facebook.

3

Find Friends on Facebook

There is no need for an introduction about Facebook. It's a huge source of information, we are connected to a lot of people, and we keep following the things that happen in our network. We get to know not only about the people in our network but also about places, movies, companies, and so on. With over 1.44 billion active users monthly, Facebook is also used as a medium to make promotions. It is being used by individuals, companies, news channels, and so on. Let's see what we can do using the Facebook Graph API.

In this chapter, we will see how to use the R package `Rfacebook`, which provides access to the Facebook Graph API from R. It includes a series of functions that allow us to extract various data about our network such as friends, likes, comments, followers, newsfeeds, and much more.

The idea behind the chapter is to learn how to pull the data from our network and use suitable techniques to convert that data into valuable information that can be used to solve a problem or a business case. We will discuss how to visualize our Facebook network and we will see some methodologies to make use of the available data to implement business cases, such as identifying the influential persons in a network, methods to detect a spam post, and finally recommend your friends what they might be interested in based on your network information.

In this chapter, we will cover the following topics:

- Creating an app on the Facebook platform
- Installation and authentication of the `Rfacebook` package
- Basic analysis of your network

- Network analysis and visualization
- Getting Facebook page data
- Measuring **Click-through rate (CTR)** performance for a page
- Trending topics
- Spam detection
- Influencers
- Order of stories on users' timeline
- Recommendations to friends

 While the Facebook Graph API allows us to get so much useful data with the recent updates to Version 2.0, Facebook deprecated few of the functionalities. In Version 1.0, we were able to download the complete details about all our friends, and search based on keywords, but now we can access just our friend's data if the details are publicly available or if they are using our app.

A Facebook app is required to perform the authentication and access the data. We will see the steps involved in creation of an app and the authentication process to enable the data access in detail.

Creating an app on the Facebook platform

In this section, we will cover the steps involved in creating a Facebook app to connect to the Facebook Graph API. Version 2 of the API deprecated a lot of features compared to Version 1, but still Facebook provides access to a lot of public data that can be used to solve various use cases.

In order to create a Facebook app, go to `https://developers.facebook.com/`, register as a Facebook developer, click on the **My Apps** option, and then choose **Add a New App**.

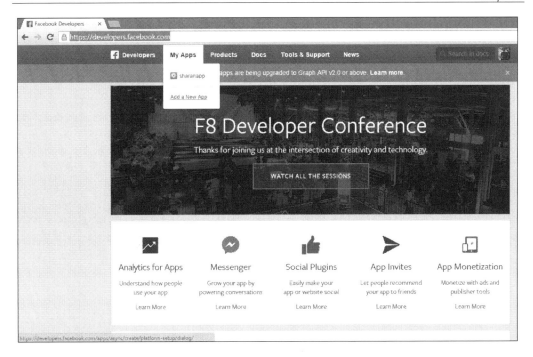

In the next window, choose **Website**, give a name to your app, and save the details by clicking on the **Create New Facebook App ID** button. In the next window, choose an appropriate category for your app and confirm by clicking on the **Create App ID** button.

Now, our app is created. Click on **Skip Quick Start** on the top-right corner of the page and move directly to the **App Settings** page. We will use this app to access our Facebook Graph API.

 Kindly ensure Rtools of version 32 is installed before loading the package devtools.

Rfacebook package installation and authentication

The Rfacebook package is authored and maintained by Pablo Barbera and Michael Piccirilli. It provides an interface to the Facebook API. It needs Version 2.12.0 or later of R and it is dependent on a few other packages, such as httr, rjson, and httpuv. Before starting, make sure those packages are installed. It is preferred to have Version 0.6 of the httr package installed.

Installation

We will now install the Rfacebook packages. We can download and install the latest package from GitHub using the following code and load the package using the library function. On the other hand, we can also install the Rfacebook package from the CRAN network. One prerequisite for installing the package using the function install_github is to have the package devtools loaded into the R environment. The code is as follows:

```
install.packages("devtools")
library(devtools)
install_github("Rfacebook", "pablobarbera", subdir="Rfacebook")
library(Rfacebook)
```

After installing the Rfacebook package for connecting to the API, make an authentication request. This can be done via two different methods. The first method is by using the access token generated for the app, which is short-lived (valid for two hours); on the other hand, we can create a long-lasting token using the OAuth function.

Let's first create a temporary token. Go to https://developers.facebook.com/tools/explorer, click on **Get Token**, and select the required user data permissions.

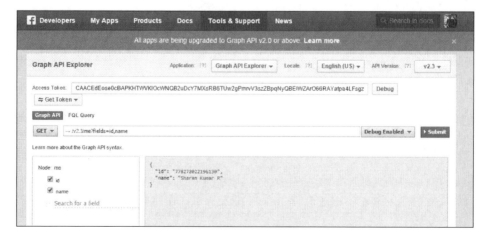

The Facebook Graph API explorer will open with an access token. This access token will be valid for two hours. The status of the access token as well as the scope can be checked by clicking on the **Debug** button. Once the tokens expire, we can regenerate a new token.

Now, we can access the data from R using the following code. The access token generated using the link should be copied and passed to the token variable. The use of username in the function `getUsers` is deprecated in the latest Graph API; hence, we are passing the ID of a user. You can get your ID from the same link that was used for token generation. This function can be used to pull the details of any user, provided the generated token has the access. Usually, access is limited to a few users with a public setting or those who use your app. It is also based on the items selected in the user data permission check page during token generation. In the following code, paste your token inside the double quotes, so that it can be reused across the functions without explicitly mentioning the actual token.

```
token<- "XXXXXXXXX"
```

A closer look at how the package works

The `getUsers` function using the token will hit the Facebook Graph API. Facebook will be able to uniquely identify the users as well as the permissions to access information. If all the check conditions are satisfied, we will be able to get the required data.

Copy the token from the mentioned URL and paste it within the double quotes. Remember that the token generated will be active only for two hours. Use the `getUsers` function to get the details of the user. Earlier, the `getUsers` function used to work based on the Facebook friend's name as well as ID; in API Version 2.0, we cannot access the data using the name. Consider the following code for example:

```
token<- "XXXXXXXXX"
me<- getUsers("778278022196130", token, private_info = TRUE)
```

Then, the details of the user, such as name and hometown, can be retrieved using the following code:

```
me$name
```

The output is also mentioned for your reference:

```
[1] "Sharan Kumar R"
```

For the following code:

```
me$hometown
```

The output is as follows:

```
[1] "Chennai, Tamil Nadu"
```

Now, let's see how to create a long-lasting token. Open your Facebook app page by going to `https://developers.facebook.com/apps/` and choosing your app.

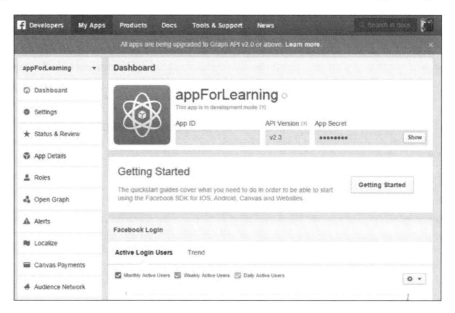

On the **Dashboard** tab, you will be able to see the **App ID** and **Secret Code** values. Use those in the following code.

```
require("Rfacebook")
fb_oauth<-
fbOAuth(app_id="11",app_secret="XX",extended_permissions = TRUE)
```

On executing the preceding statements, you will find the following message in your console:

```
Copy and paste into Site URL on Facebook App Settings:
http://localhost:1410/
When done, press any key to continue...
```

Copy the URL displayed and open your Facebook app; on the **Settings** tab, click on the **Add Platform** button and paste the copied URL in the **Site URL** text box. Make sure to save the changes.

Then, return to the R console and press any key to continue, you will be prompted to enter your Facebook username and password. On completing that, you will return to the R console. If you find the following message, it means your long-lived token is ready to use. When you get the completion status, you might not be able to access any of the information. It is advisable to use the `OAuth` function a few minutes after creation of the Facebook application.

```
Authentication complete.
Authentication successful.
```

After successfully authenticating, we can save it and load on demand using the following code:

```
save(fb_oauth, file="fb_oauth")
load("fb_oauth")
```

When it is required to automate a few things or to use `Rfacebook` extensively, it will be very difficult as the tokens should be generated quite often. Hence, it is advisable to create a long-lasting token to authenticate the user, and then save it. Whenever required, we can just load it from a local file.

Note that Facebook authentication might take several minutes. Hence, if your authentication fails on the retry, please wait for some time before pressing any key and check whether you have installed the `httr` package Version 0.6. If you continue to experience any issues in generating the token, then it's not a problem. We are good to go with the temporary token.

Exercise

Create an app in Facebook and authenticate by any one of the methods discussed.

A basic analysis of your network

In this section, we will discuss how to extract Facebook network of friends and some more information about the people in our network.

After completing the app creation and authentication steps, let's move forward and learn to pull some basic network data from Facebook. First, let's find out which friends we have access to, using the following command in R. Let's use the temporary token for accessing the data:

```
token<- "XXXXXXXXX"
friends<- getFriends(token, simplify = TRUE)
head(friends) # To see few of your friends
```

The preceding function will return all our Facebook friends whose data is accessible. Version 1 of the API would allow us to download all the friends' data by default. But in the new version, we have limited access. Since we have set `simplify` as `TRUE`, we will pull only the username and their Facebook ID. By setting the same parameter to `FALSE`, we will be able to access additional data such as gender, location, hometown, profile picture, relationship status, and full name.

We can use the function `getUsers` to get additional information about a particular user. The following information is available by default: gender, location, and language. We can, however, get some additional information such as relationship status, birthday, and the current location by setting the parameter `private_info` to `TRUE`:

```
friends_data<- getUsers(friends$id, token, private_info = TRUE)
table(friends_data$gender)
```

The output is as follows:

```
female    male
     5      21
```

We can also find out the language, location, and relationship status. The commands to generate the details as well as the respective outputs are given here for your reference:

```
#Language
table(substr(friends_data$locale, 1, 2))
```

The output is as follows:

```
en
26
```

The code to find the location is as follows:

```
# Location (Country)
  table(substr(friends_data$locale, 4, 5))
```

The output is as follows:

```
GB US
 1 25
```

Here's the code to find the relationship status:

```
# Relationship Status
table(friends_data$relationship_status)
```

Here's the output:

```
Engaged Married  Single
      1       1       3
```

Now, let's see what things were liked by us in Facebook. We can use the function `getLikes` to get the like data. In order to know about your *likes* data, specify user as `me`. The same function can be used to extract information about our friends, in which case we should pass the user's Facebook ID. This function will provide us with a list of Facebook pages liked by the user, their ID, name, and the website associated with the page. We can even restrict the number of results retrieved by setting a value to the parameter n. The same function will be used to get the likes of people in our network; instead of the keyword `me`, we should give the Facebook ID of those users. *Remember we can only access data of people with accessibility from our app.* The code is as follows:

```
likes<- getLikes(user="me", token=token)
head(likes)
```

After exploring the use of functions to pull data, let's see how to use the Facebook Query Language using the function `getFQL`, which can be used to pass the queries. The following query will get you the list of friends in your network:

```
friends<- getFQL("SELECT uid2 FROM friend
WHERE uid1=me()", token=token)
```

In order to get the complete details of your friends, the following query can be used. The query will return the username, Facebook ID, and the link to their profile picture. Note that we might not be able to access the complete network of friends' data, since access to data of all your friends are deprecated with Version 2.0. The code is as follows:

```
# Details about friends
```

```
Friends_details<- getFQL("SELECT uid, name, pic_square FROM user
WHERE uid = me() OR uid IN (SELECT uid2 FROM friend
WHERE uid1 = me())", token=token)
```

In order to know more about the Facebook Query Language, check out the following link. This method of extracting the information might be preferred by people familiar with query language. It can also help extract data satisfying only specific conditions (https://developers.facebook.com/docs/technical-guides/fql).

Exercise

Download your Facebook network and do an exploration analysis on the languages your friends speak, places where they live, the total number of pages they have liked, and their marital status. Try all these with the Facebook Query Language as well.

Network analysis and visualization

So far, we used a few functions to get the details about our Facebook profile as well as friends' data. Let's see how to get to know more about our network. Before learning to get the network data, let's understand what a network is as well as a few important concepts about the network.

Anything connected to a few other things could be a network. Everything in real life is connected to each other, for example, people, machines, events, and so on. It would make a lot of sense if we analyzed them as a network. Let's consider a network of people; here, people will be the nodes in the network and the relationship between them would be the edges (lines connecting them).

Social network analysis

The technique to study/analyze the network is called social network analysis. We will see how to create a simple plot of friends in our network in this section.

To understand the nodes (people/places/etc) in a network in social network analysis, we need to evaluate the position of the nodes. We can evaluate the nodes using centrality. Centrality can be measured using different methods like degree, betweenness, and closeness. Let's first get our Facebook network and then get to know the centrality measures in detail.

We use the function `getNetwork` to download our Facebook network. We need to mention how we would like to format the data. When the parameter `format` is set to `adj.matrix`, it will produce the data in matrix format where the people in the network would become the row names and column names of the matrix and if they are connected to each other, then the corresponding cell in the matrix will hold a value. The command is as follows:

```
network<- getNetwork(token, format="adj.matrix")
```

We now have our Facebook network downloaded. Let's visualize our network before getting to understand the centrality concept one by one with our own network. To visualize the network, we need to use the package called `igraph` in R. Since we downloaded our network in the adjacency matrix format, we will use the same function in `igraph`. We use the `layout` function to determine the placement of vertices in the network for drawing the graph and then we use the `plot` function to draw the network. In order to explore various other functionalities in these parameters, you can execute the `?<function_name>` function in RStudio and the help window will have the description of the function. Let's use the following code to load the package `igraph` into R.

```
require(igraph)
```

We will now build the graph using the function `graph.adjacency`; this function helps in creating a network graph using the adjacency matrix. In order to build a force-directed graph, we will use the function `layout.drl`. The force-directed graph will help in making the graph more readable. The commands are as follows:

```
social_graph<- graph.adjacency(network)
layout<- layout.drl(social_graph,
    options=list(simmer.attraction=0))
```

At last, we will use the `plot` function with various built in parameters to make the graph more readable. For example, we can name the nodes in our network, we can set the size of the nodes as well as the edges in the network, and we can color the graph and the components of the graph. Use the following code to see what the network looks like. The output that was plotted can be saved locally using the function `dev.copy`, and the size of the image as well as the type can be passed as a parameter to the function:

```
plot(social_graph, vertex.size=10, vertex.color="green",
vertex.label=NA,
vertex.label.cex=0.5,
edge.arrow.size=0, edge.curved=TRUE,
```

```
layout=layout.fruchterman.reingold)
dev.copy(png,filename=
"C:/Users/Sharan/Desktop/3973-03-community.png",
width=600, height=600);
dev.off ();
```

With the preceding `plot` function, my network will look like the following one. In the following network, the node labels (name of the people) have been disabled. They can be enabled by removing the `vertex.label` parameter.

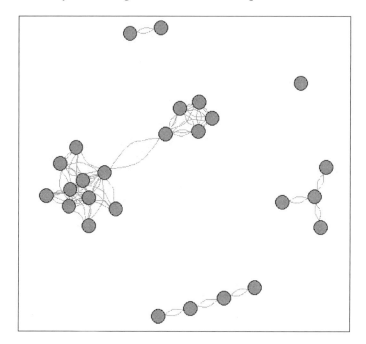

Degree

The number of direct connections a node has in a network is called the **degree**. A higher degree means that the node is connected to a lot of other nodes, which makes the nodes with a higher degree very important for various business cases. Degree can be further classified into in-degree and out-degree. To know more about the concept of networks, refer to the course *Social Network Analysis* by Lada Adamic available at coursera, which can be found at `https://www.coursera.org/course/sna`. Consider the following code to measure the degree of a network:

```
# MeasuringDegree for a network
degree(social_graph, v=V(social_graph), mode =
c("all", "out", "in", "total"),loops = TRUE, normalized = FALSE)
degree.distribution(social_graph, cumulative = FALSE)
```

The `degree` function will produce output similar to the one shown here. The `degree.distribution` function is a numeric vector of the same length as the maximum degree plus one. The first element is the relative frequency of zero degree vertices and the second element is the relative frequency of vertices with degree one and so on. The use of degree as a measure of centrality is generally not preferred because it takes into account only the nodes that are directly connected to it.

Anurup Raveendran	Samir Madhavan	Prasanna Sankaranarayanan
8	15	2
Philip Solomon	Pradeep Mohan	Alok Goel
10	2	4

 Note that the preceding screenshot is just a part of the output.

Betweenness

Betweenness is also a concept of centrality. It is calculated based on how many pairs of individuals (other nodes in the network) would have to go through you (node for which it is calculated) in order to reach one another in the minimum number of hops. The node with higher Betweenness will have a greater influence in the flow of the information. Consider the following code to measure Betweenness:

```
#Measuring Betweenness
betweenness(social_graph, v=V(social_graph), directed = TRUE,
weights = NULL, nobigint = TRUE, normalized = FALSE)
```

If our network is a directed one, then we need to set the parameter `directed` as `TRUE`. The preceding function measures the Betweenness for all the nodes in the network. If you would like to measure the Betweenness manually, it can be done using this formula:

$$C_B(i) = \sum_{j<k} P_{jk}(i) / P_{jk} \quad \text{Where } p_{jk} = \text{the number of shortest paths connecting } jk$$
$$p_{jk}(i) = \text{the number that actor } i \text{ is on}$$

The output to the preceding function will also be very similar to the `degree` function, but here we will see the Betweenness value for each of our friends in our network.

Closeness

Closeness is also a measure of centrality; how central you are (node for which it is calculated) depends on the length of the average shortest path between the measuring node and all other nodes in the network. The nodes with high closeness are very important because they are in an excellent position to monitor what's happening in the network, that is, nodes with highest visibility. This measure might not be of much use when our network has many disconnected components. Consider the following code to measure closeness:

```
# Measuring Closeness
closeness(social_graph, vids=V(social_graph), mode = c("out",
"in", "all", "total"), weights = NULL, normalized = FALSE)
```

The preceding function measures the closeness for all the nodes in the network. You can measure the closeness manually as well using the following formula:

$$C_c(i) = \left[\sum_{j=1}^{N} d(i,j)\right]^{-1}$$ Where $d(i,j)$ is the shortest distance between nodes (i) and (j)

The output to the preceding function will also be very similar to the degree function, but here we will see the closeness score for each of our friends in our network.

Cluster

Cluster is a measure of extent to which the nodes in the network tend to cluster with each other. We can see how many clusters there are in our network using the following function:

```
# Cluster in network
is.connected(social_graph, mode=c("weak", "strong"))
```

The first function `is.connected` is used to check whether the network is strongly clustered or not. The second function actually returns us the number of the clusters and the size of the clusters in the network.

The `clusters` function is used to identify the total number of clusters in the network. It computes the number of elements in each of the clusters, that is, the size of the cluster as well as the total number of clusters.

The nodes that are not connected to anyone else in the network will be considered as a separate cluster. Let us identify the number of clusters present in the dataset using the following code.

```
clusters(social_graph, mode=c("weak", "strong"))
```

The output is as follows:

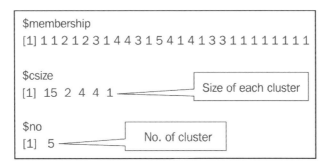

Communities

After checking the number of clusters in the network, let's check how these clusters are spread in the network. We can use the `walktrap.community` function. This function will identify the communities in the network, and we can see the communities using the `plot` function. From the output, we can clearly see the five different groups in the network, which match with the output of the cluster function. We can also check the strength of the division of network into subgroups. Networks with high modularity will have dense connections between the nodes in the subgroup. Consider the following code to plot communities:

```
# Plotting Community
network_Community<- walktrap.community(social_graph)
```

The `modularity` function is used to detect the communities in the network. It measures how modular a given division of a network graph into subgraphs is, that is, how strong a division within a network is. Networks with high a modularity score have strong connections between the nodes within their cluster (group/ community). Consider the following code to find the modularity:

```
modularity(network_Community)
plot(network_Community, social_graph, vertex.size=10,
vertex.label.cex=0.5, vertex.label=NA, edge.arrow.size=0,
edge.curved=TRUE,layout=layout.fruchterman.reingold)
```

The output is as follows:

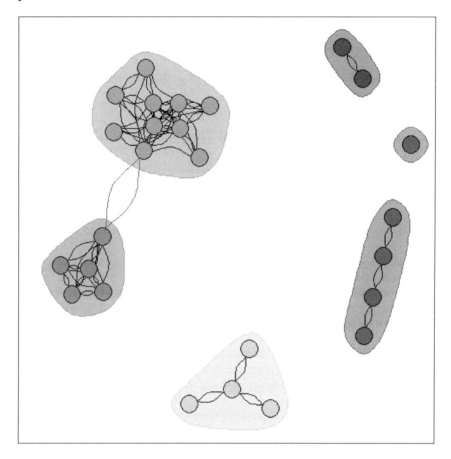

So far, we saw some of the concepts of social network analysis. Social network analysis is a huge area of research, and it is beyond the scope of this book. But at an abstract level, it helps us to detect the various communities in a network, identifying the people at the center of the network and measuring the shortest distance between two people in a network. The various business cases that could be solved using the social network analysis are as follows:

- Tracing the source of information dissemination as well as the opinion formation
- Identifying the most influential person in a network for social media campaign targeting
- For human resource, identifying the barrier for internal communication
- How fast can a flu spread?

Exercise

- Identify the most influential person in your network.
- Identify the top ten people with the highest degree in your network.
- Identify the number of clusters in your network.
- Identify people who have the best centrality score based on degree, Betweenness, and Closeness. Use equal weightage to all of them and compute a single cumulative score.

Getting Facebook page data

Facebook is not only used by individuals but also by many businesses. Most of the businesses create a Facebook page to advertise about their company and to display their products, offers, and related content. Hence, it becomes really important to check what kinds of posts are liked by the user, perform experimentation with different content, and identify the content that results in a follower's engagement.

Let's see how to get the contents of a page. First, we need to get the name of the page. We can get this from the URL of the page. Let's take TED as an example; from the URL, we know that the name of the page is TED.

We use the function `getPage` to get the contents posted in TED's page. For proper functioning of the function, ensure that Version 0.6 of the `httr` package is loaded in the R environment. Unlike Facebook friends' data, it is not necessary to like the page in order to pull the data. We can pull the data from any page provided the page, as well as the content, is public. The code is as follows:

```
######### Facebook Page data
page<- getPage("TED", token, n = 50)
head(page, n=2)
```

The output is as follows:

```
> head(page, n=2)
      from_id from_name                                                                                                                        message
1 29092950651       TED "Real faith has no easy answers. It involves an ongoing struggle, a continual questioning of what we think we know."
2 29092950651       TED                                                                       what podcasts would you add to this list?
           created_time type                      link                       id likes_count comments_count shares_count
1 2015-05-24T16:22:04+0000 link http://t.ted.com/z8bnA7r 29092950651_10155571557845652         874             39          379
2 2015-05-24T15:36:36+0000 link http://t.ted.com/902koHM 29092950651_10155571291350652        2291            269         1391
>
```

The preceding function will pull 50 posts (not necessarily latest) from the TED page. Using the `head` function, we can see the details of the top rows of the resultant dataset. The success of a Facebook post is usually measured by the number of people who liked it and the number of people who commented about it, as it tells us how much engagement was triggered by the post as well as the number of times it has been shared by different people on their Facebook profile. All these details can be obtained from the preceding function. With Version 1.0 of the Facebook Graph API, we were able to search for a post with a keyword, but that feature has been deprecated with Version 2.0. Hence, now we need to know the ID or the name of the post if we want to get the details of a particular post. The commands are as follows:

```
#Let's get the detail about the post which had the maximum number of
likes.
# Page with maximum likes
page[which.max(page$likes_count), ]
```

Out of the 50 posts that we have pulled from the TED page, we got the post that had the maximum number of likes. From the output, we see that the most popular post had about 20,000 likes:

```
> page[which.max(page$likes_count), ]
      from_id from_name
44 29092950651       TED

message
44 "You don't think in depression that you've put on a gray veil and are seeing the world through the haze of a bad mood. You think that the veil ha
s been taken away, the veil of happiness, and that now you're seeing truly." - Andrew Solomon
           created_time type                      link                       id likes_count comments_count shares_count
44 2015-05-17T22:20:15+0000 link http://t.ted.com/IQlhevq 29092950651_10155534196980652       20812            576         9546
>
```

Now, let's see what kind of details are captured and what kind of analysis can be performed that would help us to measure the impact.

Exercise

- Identify the top performing post as well as the lowest performing post and explore the difference between them
- Download the most recent 1000 posts from a page and see what time those posts are mostly made

Trending topics

The concept of trending topics is quite popular. We can see the trending topics in news websites, Twitter, and so on. But how can we identify the trending topic for a particular Facebook page or a group of Facebook pages? Let's see how it can be done in detail.

Trend analysis

Now, we will see how to learn which posts are doing well in recent times. After selecting the page that we are planning to do some analysis for, we will filter the posts' data based on a time range. Let's consider the same TED page and filter the recent data and see the posts that were popular:

```
# Most trending posts
page<- getPage("TED", token, n = 500)
head(page, n=20)
```

We pull the interactions, that is, messages posted in a page using the getPage function. In the following code, we are filtering the data. We are pulling the data that was posted after April 1, 2015. Then, we order the post based on the number of likes, and we use the head function to display the top posts and their details. The code is as follows:

```
pageRecent<- page[which(page$created_time> "2015-04-01"), ]
top<- pageRecent[order(- pageRecent$likes),]
head(top, n=10)
```

Here's the output:

```
    from_id from_name                                                           message              created_time  type
221 29092950651       TED                     At this school, kids can climb to class: 2015-04-24T16:20:32+0000  link
155 29092950651       TED watch a beautiful talk on happiness: http://t.ted.com/xrwdcbs 2015-05-03T16:12:52+0000 photo
                                                                                    link                               id likes_count
221                                                          http://t.ted.com/znts50P 29092950651_10155447292600652       39824
155 https://www.facebook.com/TED/photos/a.10152228735380652.917907.29092950651/10155482960520652/?type=1 29092950651_10155482960520652       39010
    comments_count shares_count
221            994        12072
155            221        11521
> |
```

The preceding screenshot is just a part of the output.

We can use the `which` function in order to filter the recent posts made in the TED page. After filtering the recent posts, we can use the `order` function to sort all the posts based on popularity. In this case, we are considering the number of likes for the post as a proxy for a good post. By using the minus symbol, we are sorting the post in descending order. Hence, the top post will come at the top.

In order to check the trend for the top posts, we will obtain the preceding details on a daily basis and combine them using the function `rbind`, and finally, filter the posts based on the post ID as well as the date to check the trend for the posts. This will be helpful to know if there has been any spike in the popularity of a post.

If we increase the granularity of the analysis by repeating the preceding exercise more frequently, say every hour. We would be able to see the patterns of interaction. For example, we would be able to see the time when the interactions of the followers are highest.

Exercise

- Identify the trending post for a different group.
- How long does the post remain on top? This could be achieved only by continuously monitoring the data for a few days/weeks.

Influencers

Having seen the details of the post, let's see how to learn about the people who comment and like these posts and to check if there is anyone who is more influential. For doing such an analysis, first we need to pull the data about the user interaction in a particular post.

Based on a single post

Let's take the most recent post and pull all the user comments using the function `getPost`. For each of those comments, let's see how many people liked it using the following code:

```
post_id<- head(page$id, n = 1)   ## ID of most recent post
post<- getPost(post_id, token, n = 1000, likes = TRUE,
comments = TRUE)
head(post$comments, n=2)
```

The output is as follows:

```
     from_id        from_name                                                      message          created_time likes_count
1   634288236162 Tommy McCracken Hopefully Will Smith is still alive, at that point. 2015-05-25T17:59:55+0000          29
2 939236089436290 Sandra Munsters                      That's what hammers are for. 2015-05-25T17:58:27+0000          21
                                          id
1 10155576523130652_10155576541395652
2 10155576523130652_10155576535670652
```

```
samppost<- post$comments
```

The preceding command will copy all the comments of a particular post. After that, in order to check the user who had the maximum likes, we can write a query using the function sqldf. First, we need to import the package sqldf and write a query using sqldf. Since we are interested in only those users who had the most number of likes, we are pulling only the username and the number of likes for the various comments by the user. Then, we will arrange them in descending order to know the top users of this post in the TED page.

```
library(sqldf)
comments <- post$comments
influentialusers<- sqldf("select from_name, sum(likes_count)
as totlikes from comments group by from_name")
head(Infusers)
head(Infusers)
influentialusers$totlikes<- as.numeric(influentialusers$totlikes)
# Sorting the users based on the number of likes they received
top<- influentialusers[order(- influentialusers$totlikes),]
head(top, n=10)
```

The output is as follows:

```
              from_name totlikes
79      Tommy McCracken       30
71      Sandra Munsters       21
40         Kevin Kelly        12
10          Brainwire        11
9           Bo Luc Lac         4
69           Ryan Baker         4
17    Cristobal Zamarron       3
43         Lindy Madsen         3
11      Brigitte Mercier       2
18 David Bravo Querido        2
>
```

Based on multiple posts

Based on a single post or a few comments, can we come to a conclusion on if a particular user is influential or not? In order to identify the overall favorite user, we will first download the comments posted in all the posts. Combine them using the `rbind` function, and finally write a SQL query using the `sqldf` function with `groupby"user name"`.

For the Facebook page TED, let's check the most influential person. We will first download the top 100 posts from the page. Convert them into a matrix so that it becomes easy to access the comments based on their position, and initialize the data frame `allcomments` as null. The code is as follows:

```
post_id<- head(page$id, n = 100)
head(post_id, n=10)
post_id<- as.matrix(post_id)
allcomments<- ""
```

In the `for` loop, we will traverse post by post and append all the comments of the posts to the data frame `allcomments`. The following `for` loop might take some time because we are consolidating thousands of comments. Finally, we will sort the users based on the number of likes they got for their comments. Hence, we get to know the most influential person in the page. The code is as follows:

```
# Collecting all the commments from all the 100 posts
for (i in 1:nrow(post_id))
{
   # Get upto 1000 comments for each post
post<- getPost(post_id[i,], token, n = 1000,
likes = TRUE, comments = TRUE)
comments<- post$comments
   # Append the comments to a single data frame
allcomments<- rbind(allcomments, comments)
}
```

Once we have consolidated all the comments, we use the `sqldf` function to aggregate the likes based on user. To know how many users have commented in the posts and in total how many liked their comments, the code is as follows:

```
# Consolidating the like for each user.
influentialusers<- sqldf("select from_name, sum(likes_count) as
totlikes from allcomments group by from_name")
influentialusers$totlikes<- as.numeric(influentialusers$totlikes)
top<- influentialusers[order(- influentialusers$totlikes),]
head(top, n=20)
```

Here's the output:

```
> head(top, n=20)
                     from_name totlikes
1674                 Be Smart.      494
3558             Darren Fearnley     465
6435               Jason de Luca    409
9998           Mary Harnishfeger    355
7644                Karen Duffin    342
8850               Levi Courtney    273
8075           Kenneth V Butland    264
5938                Iris Kirkwood   260
14263                 Tam Young     251
14835             Tricia McLaren    200
3432                Daniel Kolsi    193
4582          Eric Brent Wangner   180
4959            Francine Lorriman   173
14199             Sydney Murillo    169
14228                       TED     165
7535               Justin Bibler    160
8751                 Lee Sutton    160
13546             Shay Voncreer     152
10606             Miguel Claxton    146
14682 Todd William Ristau          138
>
```

In the same way, we can do this for a group of related pages. Getting to know the most influential person is a very useful task, that is very helpful for executing marketing campaigns and making them successful.

Exercise

Repeat the preceding example for a different page. Try implementing with different weightages. Give more weightage to shares. For the positive comments, this could be achieved by building a list of positive words and checking the comments for any word from this list. At last, give least weightage for the likes to find the influential person.

Measuring CTR performance for a page

The performance of a page can be measured by the user activity in the page and the user's interaction in the posts published in the page. Let's measure the performance for a page. When we say measuring the performance, it is by means of counting the user interaction through likes, comments, and shares.

In order to come up with a trend, we will need the timestamp data. Then, we need to consolidate the data on a monthly basis so that we can draw the time-series performance chart.

First, we need to convert the Facebook date format into R-supported date format. The following code is a function to convert the date format. We need to pass the date timestamp data to this function. The function will return the same date timestamp in R-supported format so that we can perform date operation. The code is as follows:

```
format.facebook.date<- function(datestring) {
date<- as.POSIXct(datestring,
format = "%Y-%m-%dT%H:%M:%S+0000", tz = "GMT")
}
```

Then, we need to aggregate the data on a monthly basis. The `aggregate.metric` function will aggregate the required data on a monthly basis. We will pass the likes, comments, and shares count data to this function. We would have already converted the date to the required format using the previous function. The code is as follows:

```
aggregate.metric<- function(metric) {
m<- aggregate(page[[paste0(metric, "_count")]],
list(month = page$month),
mean)
m$month<- as.Date(paste0(m$month, "-15"))
m$metric<- metric
return(m)
}
```

Then, let's see how our R code makes use of the preceding functions and to plot the performance trend. Finally, we use the `ggplot` function to plot the trend and save the plot using the function `ggsave`. The quality of image can be adjusted using the `dpi` parameter.

Use the `getPage` function to extract all the posts from the Facebook page `bimtrichy`. The number of pages to be retrieved can be altered using the parameter n. In this case, we are downloading the top 500 posts. The command is as follows:

```
page<- getPage("bimtrichy", token, n = 500)
```

We are passing the date timestamp to the function `format.facebook.date` created by us. So it will be converted to a format that would be supported by the aggregate function which will be used next. The code is as follows:

```
page$datetime<- format.facebook.date(page$created_time)
page$month<- format(page$datetime, "%Y-%m")
```

We are using the aggregate function to aggregate the number of likes, comments, and shares on a monthly basis. The code is as follows:

```
df.list<- lapply(c("likes", "comments", "shares"),
aggregate.metric)
df<- do.call(rbind, df.list)
```

We need the `ggplot2` and `scales` packages in order to make the plot. Hence, we need to load those packages using the `library` function. We plot the graph using the `ggplot` function and define a few parameters to make the graph readable. The code is as follows:

```
library(ggplot2)
library(scales)
ggplot(df, aes(x = month, y = x, group = metric))
+ geom_line(aes(color = metric))
+ scale_x_date(breaks = "years", labels = date_format("%Y"))
+ scale_y_log10("Average count per post", breaks =
c(10, 100, 1000, 10000, 50000))
+ theme_bw()
+ theme(axis.title.x = element_blank())
+ ggtitle("Facebook Page Performance")
ggsave(file="C:/Users/Sharan/Desktop/3973-format-trend.png",
dpi=500)
```

The output is as follows:

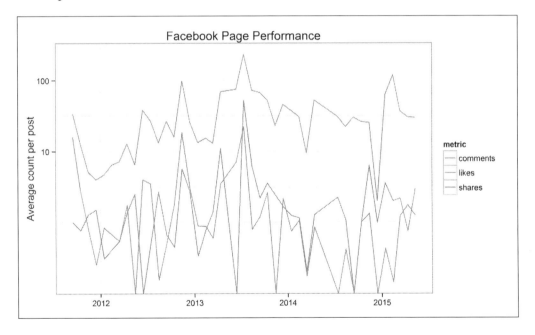

Hence, we can now see the performance trend chart. The same data can be used to plot the chart on an hourly, quarterly, or yearly basis with little modification to the existing code. Similarly, different metrics could be defined, computed, and the trend could be plotted.

Exercise

Consider a few Facebook pages; give weightages to the likes, comments, and the shares; and then compute a new score that is a weighted sum of the measures. Then, aggregate the score for each of those pages on a monthly basis and plot the trend chart to compare the performance of multiple pages over the same period of time. This will help to identify patterns in the trend. This could be done for a similar set of pages and also diverse pages.

Along with the metrics, likes, comments, and shares, try to add the number of characters in the post. Also, try to have a filter based on the type of post, which could be video, message, and so on.

Spam detection

Spam detection is an important use case to deal with. With the growing number of users, the number of spam comments/messages is also increasing. Hence, it is important to build a model or a rule engine which would be capable of identifying the fraudulent user, posting some random message.

The implementation of this algorithm would be slightly difficult because there is no direct mechanism to tag a post as spam. In this section, we will teach you to build a basic model based on certain parameters as well as users' inputs to identify a spam post. This will definitely help you to understand the concept. Any such algorithm implemented would require a constant update since the spammers too, would change their strategy.

Implementing a spam detection algorithm

The following is a simple implementation of a spam detection algorithm using logistic regression. Let's see in detail what the code does to predict the spam messages as comments in the Facebook page posts:

```
page<- getPage("beach4all", token, n = 500)
post_id<- head(page$id, n = 100)
head(post_id, n=10)
post_id<- as.matrix(post_id)
allcomments<- ""
for (i in 1:nrow(post_id))
{
post<- getPost(post_id[i,], token, n = 1000,
likes = TRUE, comments = TRUE)
```

```
comments<- post$comments
allcomments<- rbind(allcomments, comments)
}
allcomments<- as.data.frame(allcomments)
allcomments$chars<- ""
allcomments$chars<- nchar(allcomments$message)
allcomments$url<- ""
allcomments$url<- grepl(".com", allcomments$message)
allcomments$spam<- ""
train<- allcomments[1:100,]
test<- allcomments[101:nrow(allcomments),]
write.csv(train,"comment-train.csv" )
write.csv(test,"comment-test.csv")
train<- read.csv("comment-train.csv" )
test<- read.csv("comment-test.csv" )
newTrain<- train[,c("likes_count", "chars", "url", "spam")]
newTest<- test[,c("likes_count", "chars", "url", "spam")]
glm.out = glm(spam ~ ., family=binomial(logit), data=newTrain)
prediction<- predict(glm.out,newTest, type = "response")
newTest$spam<- prediction
head(newTest)
```

First, we will download the post from a Facebook page. Using the following code, we download the latest 500 Facebook posts and then we choose the top 100 posts in the page. We use the `head` function to check the dataset. The code is as follows:

```
page<- getPage("beach4all", token, n = 500)
post_id<- head(page$id, n = 100)
head(post_id, n=10)
```

The following code had already been explained under the heading `Influencers`. This code is used to collect the comments made in the post. The final data frame, `allcomments`, will hold all the comments made in the forum.

```
post_id<- as.matrix(post_id)
allcomments<- ""
for (i in 1:nrow(post_id))
{
post<- getPost(post_id[i,], token, n = 1000,
likes = TRUE, comments = TRUE)
comments<- post$comments
allcomments<- rbind(allcomments, comments)
}
allcomments<- as.data.frame(allcomments)
```

We are going to build a few more vectors that will help in predicting the spam messages. We create two empty columns named `chars` and `URL` to hold the number of characters as well as the flag to predict messages with a URL. It has been found that most spam comments contain a URL. We use the `nchar` function to count the number of characters in the comments and then the `grepl` function to identify the comments with a URL in it. The code is as follows:

```
allcomments$chars<- ""
allcomments$chars<- nchar(allcomments$message)
allcomments$url<- ""
allcomments$url<- grepl(".com", allcomments$message)
allcomments$spam<- ""
```

We now divide the dataset into `train` and `test`. The first 100 rows are used as the `train` dataset and the others are used as the `test` dataset. Then, we write the new dataset into the local system. After writing the files locally, open the training dataset, manually identify the spam rows, flag them as `1` in the `spam` column, and save it. In our case, we consider the irrelevant comments with advertisement and spam links to be a spam message. Now, we will use the new `train` dataset as a training set and hence predict the spam comments in the test dataset. The code is as follows:

```
train<- allcomments[1:100,]
test<- allcomments[101:nrow(allcomments),]
write.csv(train,"comment-train.csv" )
write.csv(test,"comment-test.csv" )
```

We will read the new dataset, where we have flagged all the comments as either spam or normal. We choose the columns `likes_count`, `chars`, `url`, and `spam` to build the prediction model. We use the `glm` function with the parameter `family=binomial(logit)` to build the logistic regression model. The logistic model that has been built is stored in `glm.out`. While making the prediction, we have to pass this model to the prediction function. Based on this model, the prediction will be made for the test dataset. The code is as follows:

```
train<- read.csv("comment-train.csv" )
test<- read.csv("comment-test.csv" )
newTrain<- train[,c("likes_count", "chars", "url", "spam")]
newTest<- test[,c("likes_count", "chars", "url", "spam")]
glm.out = glm(spam ~ ., family=binomial(logit), data=newTrain)
```

Finally, we use the `predict` function for the comments in the `test` dataset. We use the parameter `type` as `response` to make sure that the predictions fall into the range 0 to 1. Update the `test` dataset's `spam` column with the prediction. Then, we merge the predicted column with the test dataset so that we can see the people whose comments were considered as spam by our algorithm.

The code is as follows:

```
prediction<- predict(glm.out,newTest, type = "response")
newTest$spam<- prediction
head(newTest)
```

Here's the output:

```
> head(newTest, 20)
          test$from_name likes_count chars   url       spam
1           Marina Beach           1    48 FALSE 0.15067290
2         Akansha Shergil           0   379  TRUE 0.99811825
3         Akhilesh Shukla           0     6 FALSE 0.07970752
4           Lavanya Logu           0    20 FALSE 0.09099393
5          Anton Prakash           0    17 FALSE 0.08846034
6        Islam Mehreliyev           0    43  TRUE 0.94263397
7         Joseph C. Holm           0    85  TRUE 0.96207681
8           Dinesh Singd           0     9 FALSE 0.08201298
9        Islam Mehreliyev           0    43  TRUE 0.94263397
10     Reshmavenugopal Pv           0     3 FALSE 0.07746141
11         Janasheen Sam           0     8 FALSE 0.08123783
12       Islam Mehreliyev           0    43  TRUE 0.94263397
13        Akansha Shergil           0   393  TRUE 0.99837146
14       Islam Mehreliyev           0    43  TRUE 0.94263397
15         Ilakkiya Babu           1     7 FALSE 0.10402343
16            Akpnjoy Joy           0     5 FALSE 0.07895228
17          Arunima Sinha           0     3 FALSE 0.07746141
18            Jenima Raja           0    24 FALSE 0.09447355
19   Filippo Arturo Didio           0     9 FALSE 0.08201298
20    Euromanis Euromanis           0    16 FALSE 0.08763006
>
```

Now that we have the probability of the message being spam, we will decide on the threshold after preliminary analysis, based on its impact on accuracy. Values closer to 1 indicate that the probability of being spam is higher. Thus, we have built the model to predict if a comment is spam or not. The accuracy of this model could be improved by building a strong list of vectors.

Exercise

From the preceding output, we can understand that the spam messages are mostly from a few users. Hence, in the exercise, try implementing a similar algorithm but instead of predicting whether a message is spam or not, predict whether the user is a spam user or not. This could also be achieved by building the vectors that would help in making the prediction. Like the attributes such as number of comments posted, number of likes received and their ratio, a few more vectors could be built.

The order of stories on a user's home page

In Facebook, when we open the home page we see multiple newsfeeds. These newsfeed are updated continuously, let's try to imitate the same in R. The following code will sort the newsfeeds in an order based on the interactions, as well as the recency of publishing. If you face any problems here, check the version of the API and retry with the API of Version 2.3. The code is as follows:

```
newsfeed<- getNewsfeed(token, n = 200)
head(newsfeed, 20)
newsfeed$datetime<- format.facebook.date(newsfeed$created_time)
currdate<- Sys.time()
maxdiff<-
max(difftime(currdate, newsfeed$datetime, units="hours"))
newsfeed$priority<-
maxdiff - difftime(currdate, newsfeed$datetime, units="hours")
newsfeed$priority<- as.numeric(newsfeed$priority)
fnpriority<- function(x){(x-min(x))/(max(x)-min(x))}
newsfeed$priority<- fnpriority(newsfeed$priority) *100
newsfeed$plikes_count<- fnpriority(newsfeed$likes_count) *100
newsfeed$pcomments_count<-
fnpriority(newsfeed$comments_count) *100
newsfeed$pshares_count<- fnpriority(newsfeed$shares_count) *100
newsfeed$score<- newsfeed$plikes_count +
newsfeed$pcomments_count + newsfeed$pshares_count +
newsfeed$priority
newsfeed<- newsfeed[order(-newsfeed$score),]
```

We will pull the newsfeed using the function `getNewsfeed`. The parameter `n` is used to specify the number of posts to be retrieved and we use the head function to display the top rows to check the data format. The code is as follows:

```
newsfeed<- getNewsfeed(token, n = 200)
head(newsfeed, 20)
```

We will then convert the date timestamp to a format that is supported by R using the function that we had created in the previous section while detecting spam messages. We use the function `Sys.time` to get the system's current timestamp. The code is as follows:

```
newsfeed$datetime<- format.facebook.date(newsfeed$created_time)
currdate<- Sys.time()
```

In the newsfeed that we see in our Facebook home page, recency holds a significant weightage. Hence, let's also try to bring in the recency factor. Using the function `difftime`, we will get the difference between the times when the post was made as well as the current time. We inverse the values by subtracting from the maximum value so that higher values would mean the post is recent. Save these values into a new column called `priority`. The code is as follows:

```
maxdiff<-
max(difftime(currdate, newsfeed$datetime, units="hours"))
newsfeed$priority<-
maxdiff - difftime(currdate, newsfeed$datetime, units="hours")
newsfeed$priority<- as.numeric(newsfeed$priority)
```

We have computed the priority but still we might find cases where there are posts that were very recent, may be just a few seconds old, as well as posts which are months old. Hence, we will use the `fnpriority` function to normalize the values between the range 0 and 1. Then, we use the function to normalize across a few of the columns that would be used to determine the priority score. In this case, we are multiplying the resultant value with 100 to bring it to the range 0 to 100:

```
fnpriority<- function(x){(x-min(x))/(max(x)-min(x))}
newsfeed$priority<- fnpriority(newsfeed$priority) *100
newsfeed$plikes_count<- fnpriority(newsfeed$likes_count) *100
newsfeed$pcomments_count<- fnpriority(newsfeed$comments_count) *100
newsfeed$pshares_count<- fnpriority(newsfeed$shares_count) *100
```

Finally, we add up the individual scores and use the `order` function to sort all the feeds in descending order. The most important post would appear on the top. In this case, we computed the importance based on the recency as well as the number of interaction through the likes, comments, and shares:

```
newsfeed$score<- newsfeed$plikes_count +
newsfeed$pcomments_count + newsfeed$pshares_count + newsfeed$priority
newsfeed<- newsfeed[order(-newsfeed$score),]
head(newsfeed)
```

The output is as follows:

```
> head(toppages, 20)
                 from_id                      from_name  type     score
133    174446452713479  Funniest And Craziest Videos video  384.6045
142    199633956730875                 Tyrese Gibson video  219.3952
95     118306468218564                     MS Dhoni photo  206.7336
98        21785951839                         9GAG photo  152.4283
97   10152256800766541         Venkatesh Sampath photo  149.0586
21     221671794535129                     womansera photo  127.3815
15     437018853025060             Pinoy Rap Radio photo  124.8140
23       173770089577           Laughing Colours photo  121.6516
169    334718749959224                   Filmygyan photo  118.8073
68     139729956046003                   Grammarly photo  117.1519
188    334718749959224                   Filmygyan photo  114.6187
119    118306468218564                     MS Dhoni photo  114.5282
59     334718749959224                   Filmygyan photo  109.8243
190    236785033139638           The Love Page photo  107.1601
53     334718749959224                   Filmygyan photo  107.0151
47     334718749959224                   Filmygyan photo  107.0027
124       41036834883         Man vs. Wild  link  106.3964
185    144234358966231                   STUNTnews video  106.2344
55       181544941601           Chetan Bhagat photo  104.7491
108       19787703062           Save the Tiger photo  103.5861
>
```

Hence, we have come up with a basic approach to replicate the stories to be displayed in our home page. We will also work on a few aspects to improve the order of the posts, and make sure that the posts that appear on top are most likely the ones which we might like.

Exercise

For each of the posts that are pulled using the Newsfeed function, get the post ID and then identify the number of comments, likes, and shares by friends. This could be achieved by getting our friends details and comparing with those of the posts. Then, use these parameters as well to compute the score. The posts that have more interaction from our friends would most likely to be our favorite.

Recommendations to friends

The objective of this chapter is to recommend to your friend, pages that they might like. We will build this recommendation using the Apriori algorithm. The following code will be useful for building the recommendation model. It makes use of the Apriori algorithm to build, generate the rules, and hence extract the patterns in the data that can be used as recommendation. Let's understand the code in detail:

```
friends<- getFriends(token, simplify = TRUE)
head(friends, 26)
friend1<- getLikes("500637447", n = 100, token)
friend2<- getLikes("505108142", n = 100, token)
friend1$user <- "friend1"
friend2$user <- "friend2"
friendlikedata<- rbind(friend1, friend2)
head(friendlikedata)
forRecc<- friendlikedata[,c("user", "id")]
write.csv(forRecc,"C:/Users/Sharan/Desktop/Chapter 3/forRecc.csv",
row.names = FALSE, col.names = NA)
library(arules)
data = read.transactions(file="C:/Users/Sharan/Desktop/Chapter
3/forRecc.csv", rm.duplicates= FALSE,
format="single",sep=",",cols =c(1,2));
head(data, 10)
nrow(data)
inspect(data)
rules<- apriori(data,parameter = list(sup = 0.2, conf = 0.001,
target="rules", minlen=3, maxlen=5));
inspect(rules);
itemFrequencyPlot(data)
image(data)
```

We use the `getFriends` function to get the details of the friends in our network. Once you have completed this step, we can extract the likes of friends one by one using the user's Facebook ID. In order to map the likes to the user, we create a user column and name it with our friend's name. Once all the friend's details are extracted, we combine them using the `rbind` function. In order to build the recommendation using Apriori, we need only the username and the pages they like. Hence, select just these columns and then write it in a local machine. The code is as follows:

```
friends<- getFriends(token, simplify = TRUE)
head(friends, 26)
friend1<- getLikes("500637447", n = 100, token)
friend2<- getLikes("505108142", n = 100, token)
friend1$user <- "friend1"
friend2$user <- "friend2"
friendlikedata<- rbind(friend1, friend2)
head(friendlikedata)
forRecc<- friendlikedata[,c("user", "id")]
write.csv(forRecc,"C:/Users/Sharan/Desktop/Chapter 3/forRecc.csv",
row.names = FALSE, col.names = NA)
```

We are going to build the rules using the `arules` package. For the first time, you have to install the package using the code `install.packages`. Load the package using the `library` function. The data has to be read using the `read.transactions` function so that the `apriori` function will understand the data. Then, we will inspect the data using the `inspect` function. It will show us the user and the pages in pairs, and we can generate the rules using the `apriori` function:

```
Install.packages("arules")
library(arules)
data = read.transactions(file="C:/Users/Sharan/Desktop/Chapter
3/forRecc.csv", rm.duplicates= FALSE,
format="single",sep=",",cols =c(1,2));
head(data, 10)
inspect(data)
```

Now that we understand more about the parameters used in the `apriori` function, the parameter support, `sup`, is the percentage of the population that satisfies the rule, while the parameter confidence, `conf`, is the percentage in which the consequent is also satisfied. We have set the threshold for these parameters. Try adjusting these parameters' thresholds so that we are able to generate a sufficient number of rules. We can check the number of rules generated using the `inspect` function:

```
rules<- apriori(data,parameter = list(sup = 0.2, conf = 0.001,
target="rules", minlen=3, maxlen=5));
inspect(rules);
```

The output is as follows:

```
> inspect(rules);
    lhs                     rhs              support confidence lift
1   {1.40113E+14,
     1.4708E+14}   => {3.39694E+11}     0.2          1.00 3.75
2   {1.4708E+14,
     3.39694E+11} => {1.40113E+14}      0.2          1.00 3.75
3   {1.40113E+14,
     3.39694E+11} => {1.4708E+14}       0.2          0.75 3.75
4   {1.08167E+14,
     4.47287E+14} => {1.40113E+14}      0.2          1.00 3.75
5   {1.40113E+14,
     4.47287E+14} => {1.08167E+14}      0.2          1.00 5.00
6   {1.08167E+14,
     1.40113E+14} => {4.47287E+14}      0.2          1.00 5.00
7   {1.08167E+14,
     4.47287E+14} => {3.39694E+11}      0.2          1.00 3.75
8   {3.39694E+11,
     4.47287E+14} => {1.08167E+14}      0.2          1.00 5.00
9   {1.08167E+14,
     3.39694E+11} => {4.47287E+14}      0.2          1.00 5.00
10  {1.40113E+14,
     4.47287E+14} => {3.39694E+11}      0.2          1.00 3.75
11  {3.39694E+11,
     4.47287E+14} => {1.40113E+14}      0.2          1.00 3.75
12  {1.40113E+14,
     3.39694E+11} => {4.47287E+14}      0.2          0.75 3.75
13  {1.08167E+14,
```

 Note that preceding screenshot is just a part of the output.

Reading the output

The output produced by the Apriori algorithm might not be self-explanatory. Let's see what it means. Those people who like the pages in the column lhs are most likely to like the page in the column rhs. We also get to know the support, as well as the confidence, for the rules generated. The lift ratio is the confidence of the rule divided by the confidence, assuming the independence of the consequent from the antecedent. A lift ratio higher than 1 suggests that there is a strong association, which means the rule generated is useful. For recommendations to the people, first, filter the users based on the pages in the column lhs and recommend them the pages in the column rhs.

Exercise

Build a recommendation system to recommend friends to your network. In our existing application, we are tagging the people to the pages that they liked. In this case, we should tag the people to the friends. Once the data has been prepared, the other approach will be similar. In order to execute this, we would need to get the token authenticated using OAuth.

Other business cases

So far, we have implemented some of the business cases. Let's see some of the other possible business cases that could be solved using the Facebook data:

1. A well-established company can use Facebook data to select the people whom they can use for the social media campaign, such as providing offers so that they could reach these people faster.

2. Identify how the reviews of the product are across different zones among people speaking different languages, people belonging to different social groups, and so on.

3. How we can merge two different communities in our network who do not have any single attribute in common.

4. What is the time when the interactions in your network are high? Is there any difference in behavior between gender, location, and qualification of the people in the network?

Summary

In this chapter, we covered the sequential steps involved in the creation of a Facebook app and used the authentication details to connect to the Facebook Graph API. We also discussed how to use the various functions implemented in the `Rfacebook` package.

This chapter covers the important techniques that helps in performing vital network analysis and also enlightens us about the wide range of business problems that could be addressed with the Facebook data. It gives us a glimpse of the great potential for implementation of various analyses.

We also discussed the trending topics, measuring CTR performance of a page, methodology to detect spam messages, identifying the influencers and providing recommendations to the users on pages to like, and much more.

In the next chapter we will discuss accessing the data from Instagram using its API and solve interesting use-cases such as identifying the most popular users and destinations. We will also explore implementation of a few machine learning techniques such as clustering and recommendation systems.

4
Finding Popular Photos on Instagram

Instagram is not just a platform for sharing photos and videos; with more than 300 million active users, it has become a popular platform for marketing. It becomes absolutely necessary for the brands and corporations to track the performance of various activities and users on Instagram to keep them ahead of the competition.

In this chapter, we will explore ways to get some interesting stats from the Instagram platform. Using the package instaR v0.1.4, we will pull the data and use the analytics capabilities in R, to explore and answer interesting questions. Some of the data that we will be extracting in this chapter will be public media from a specific hashtag, location, or user, and we will also get user profile information, followers, and following details. We can also get some of the picture details such as the likes, comments, or captions used while posting; picture type, and much more.

The objective of this chapter is to use the aforementioned data and get some really interesting metrics on users, brands, and location data, based on their activities on Instagram which solves some business use cases such as identifying popular personalities, identifying popular destinations, and providing recommendations to celebrities on the users they might be interested in following.

In this chapter, we will cover the following topics:

- Creating an app on the Instagram platform
- Installation and authentication of the instaR package
- Accessing data from R
- Building a dataset
- Popular personalities
- Finding the most popular destination

- Clustering the pictures
- Recommendations to the users
- Business cases

Creating an app on the Instagram platform

We need to register our application with Instagram in order to access the data. In order to register an application, we need to create an Instagram account, which can be created only from a mobile device. Here are the steps involved in creating an application on Instagram.

After creating an Instagram account, open the URL `https://instagram.com/developer/`:

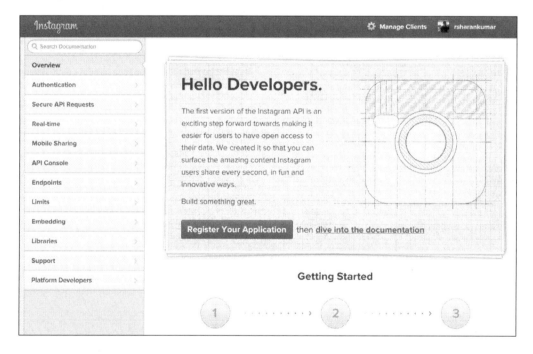

Click on the **Register Your Application** button to create a new client and fill in the following details. In the **Redirect URL** textbox, type in `http://localhost:1410/`; this is the call back URL that Instagram will return to after successful authentication. After filling in all the relevant details, click on the **Register** button at the bottom of the page:

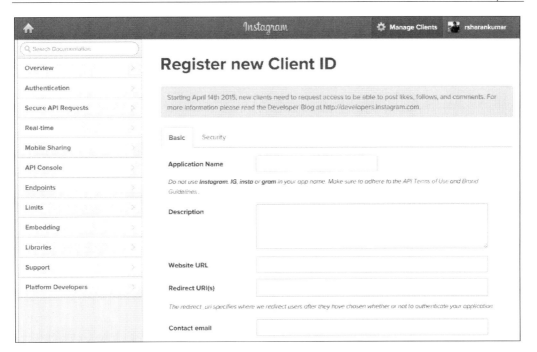

On completion of the preceding steps, the app is created and the client information such as the `OAuth`, `Client ID`, and the `Secret Key`, will be generated and can be accessed through the link **Manage Clients**. Remember to keep the information safe. We will use the Client ID and the Client Secret key to authenticate and connect to Instagram from R, by doing so, we get better accessibility to the data. We can edit the client details or reset the ID and password using the **EDIT** option in the following page:

Installation and authentication of the instaR package

The R package `instaR` is authored and maintained by Pablo Barbera and it helps R users to access the Instagram API through R. This package provides a series of functions to access information from Instagram.

We can install the latest `instaR` package directly from the GitHub repository using the following code and load the package into R using the `library` function. The package `devtools` is required in order to install directly from GitHub:

```
library(devtools)
install_github("pablobarbera/instaR/instaR")
library(instaR)
```

After installing the required package for enabling the access to the Instagram API, we will proceed to make the authentication process from R. In the following code, the variable `app_id` holds the actual **Client ID** of your app and the variable `app_secret` holds the **Client Secret**. Using the function `instaOAuth`, we generate the access token that makes it possible to make an authenticated call to the Instagram API. The token can be saved locally in the system so that it can be reused in the future:

```
app_id<- "<<paste your Client ID here>>"
app_secret<- "<<paste your key here>>"
token<- instaOAuth(app_id, app_secret)
```

On executing the preceding statement, you will find the following message in the R console:

```
Copy and paste into 'OAuthredirect_uri' on Instagram App Settings:
http://localhost:1410/
When done, press any key to continue...
```

If the redirect URL is already specified while creating the app in Instagram, you can continue by pressing any key; the authentication would happen in the browser and on successful authentication, the following message will be shown:

```
Waiting for authentication in browser...
Press Esc/Ctrl + C to abort
Authentication complete.
Authentication successful.
```

Now we are good to proceed with the data acquisition. There are multiple functions that will help us in getting the data. We will be going through it in detail in the next section.

Exercise:

Revoke the access to the app and try to access the data from R using the previous authentication.

Accessing data from R

The Instagram API provides access to some amazing content published on Instagram. It uses the OAuth 2.0 protocol for authentication and authorization as explained in the previous section. Let's see the functions present in the package instaR, which enables us to download data from R.

Searching public media for a specific hashtag

The function searchInstagram allows the users to download the public media posted on Instagram with a specific hashtag:

```
MachuPicchu<- searchInstagram("MachuPicchu", token,
n=10, folder="MachuPicchu")
```

The preceding code will return the recent public media posts on Instagram with the hashtag MachuPicchu, and the media files will be downloaded in a folder named MachuPicchu (as specified in the preceding code) in the current working directory of R. The working directory of R can be changed using the function setwd(). You can explore the content downloaded using the below code. The function names will give the various columns present in the data:

```
names(MachuPicchu)
```

The output is as follows:

```
 [1]  "type"           "longitude"        "latitude"       "location_name"
 [5]  "location_id"    "comments_count"   "filter"         "created_time"
 [9]  "link"           "likes_count"      "image_url"      "caption"
[13]  "username"       "user_id"          "user_fullname"  "id"
```

The function head shows the snapshot of the output:

```
head(MachuPicchu,2)
```

The output is as follows:

```
> head(MachuPicchu,2)
   type longitude latitude location_name location_id comments_count filter
1 image  72.54463 13.16512  Machu Picchu    482899168              1 Normal
2 image  72.54503 13.16221          <NA>           NA              3 Normal
        created_time                             link likes_count
1 2015-07-01 06:44:52 https://instagram.com/p/4kyBghPsS9/          43
2 2015-06-17 23:49:42 https://instagram.com/p/4CkLVat6qH/         312

image_url
1  https://scontent.cdninstagram.com/hphotos-xfa1/t51.2885-15/e15/11417288_4044349
618805852_n.jpg
2 https://scontent.cdninstagram.com/hphotos-xpa1/t51.2885-15/e15/10012466_86365378
628253868_n.jpg
                                            caption       username
1 Falta muito pras próximas férias? #nofilter #machupicchu rodrigocaina_
2         #WanderlustQueenP #PeruMythologyTrip #machupicchu       pupp_ns
    user_id      user_fullname                                     id
1 368489016 Rodrigo Cainã <U+26A1><U+FE0F> 10191594216551067649_368489016
2  33253561            <U+E10E>Queen P  100952837506987891919_33253561
> |
```

Searching public media from a specific location

We can also download the public media with a specific hashtag from a particular location. To the preceding code, we will add the location filter to make sure that the public media was posted from that particular location. This can be achieved using the function searchInstagram along with the location parameters. We can get the latitude and longitude of a location from Google maps by zooming in to the location, right-clicking, and selecting the option **What's here?**. The code is as follows:

```
MachuPicchu<- searchInstagram("MachuPicchu", token, n=10,
  lat= 13.1633, lng= 72.5456, distance=1000, folder="MachuPicchu")
```

In the preceding code, the latitude and the longitude specified correspond, to the location of MachuPicchu. The parameter distance allows us to extract the media content posted within a radius of 1000 meters, which can be increased up to a distance of 5000 meters.

The function searchInstagram returns the content that is up to 7 days old only, and it allows us to filter based on Hashtag or Location, or both.

Extracting public media of a user

Using the function `getUserMedia`, we can download the public media of a particular user. We will use the function to download the public media contents posted by the user `instagram`. Using the following code, we download the latest 100 public posts by the user `instagram`. Alternatively, we can also download the content by using the user's Instagram ID. The code is as follows:

```
instag <- getUserMedia("instagram", token, n=100,
folder="instagram")
```

The preceding function will download the content to a folder `instagram` in the current working directory of R. The following code is used to get an idea about the data:

```
names(instag)
head(instag)
```

The structure of the data downloaded will be similar to what we saw in the previous section.

Extracting user profile

In order to extract the basic user profile, we can use the function `getUser`. We need to pass the username and the token as parameters to this function. This function provides us with the basic profile details such as username, basic biodata, website (if available), link to the profile picture, complete username, media published, and followed by, as well as the number of people the user follows. Using the following function, we get the profile information of *Barack Obama*:

```
usr<- getUser("barackobama", token)
head(usr)
```

The output is as follows:

```
> head(usr)
    username                                                bio
1 barackobama This account is run by Organizing for Action staff.
              website
1 http://barackobama.com
                                                    profile_picture
1 https://instagramimages-a.akamaihd.net/profiles/profile_10206720_75sq_1380839853.jpg
    full_name media_count followed_by follows
1 Barack Obama        183     4166366      12
>
```

Getting followers

To know about the followers of a particular profile, we can use the function `getFollowers`. Similar to the `getUser` function, we need to pass the user's Instagram account name and the token for authentication. The code is as follows:

```
instaf<- getFollowers("instagram", token)
```

This function not only extracts the name of the followers, but also the profile information of the followers. We use the function `names` to get the details on the various variables extracted using `getFollowers`. This function might not extract the complete list of the followers if the number of followers is huge, but it will extract the recent followers:

```
names(instaf)
```

The output is as follows:

```
> names(instaf)
[1] "username"       "bio"           "website"        "profile_picture"
[5] "full_name"      "id"
>
```

 This code might run for few minutes as it is downloading details of a large number of followers.

The `getFollowers` function extracts the data in the data frame format. We can check the data using the function `head`. We have extracted the followers of the account `instagram`. We can use the function `nrow` to get to know about the number of follower's details downloaded by the function `getFollowers`. In the previous case, we extracted the basic profile details of about 521,851 followers of the account `instagram`, whose details were available as public. The code is as follows:

```
head(instaf,2)
```

The output is as follows:

```
> head(instaf,2)
          username bio website
1 aditya_shettigar  NA      NA
2          ismachg  NA      NA

profile_picture
1  https://igcdn-photos-c-a.akamaihd.net/hphotos-ak-xfa1/t51.2885-19/11242625_1106480702
701234_794638759_a.jpg
2 https://igcdn-photos-c-a.akamaihd.net/hphotos-ak-xfp1/t51.2885-19/11005104_13871689215
98970_1174694445_a.jpg
                full_name        id
1         Aditya Shettigar 612034694
2 ismary<U+2665> venezolana 654673380
>
```

For the following code:

```
nrow(instaf)
```

The output is as follows:

```
[1] 521851
```

Who does the user follow?

We have already seen how to extract details about the followers. Now, we will see how to extract the details about the people/accounts that the users follow. This can be achieved using the function getFollows and the same two parameters. This function will extract the data in the data frame format. We can check a sample of the data using the function head.

The following function extracts the basic details of the people/accounts who are followed by the account instagram. We can use the function nrow to know about the number of people whose information was extracted. In our case, we were able to extract basic profile details of 429 people. The code is as follows:

```
instaff<- getFollows("instagram", token)
head(instaff,3)
```

The output is as follows:

```
> head(instaff,3)
        username bio website
1 freegrassfarmer   NA      NA
2    themertailor   NA      NA
3      giopastori   NA      NA

profile_picture
1                              https://instagramimages-a.akamaihd.net/profiles/profile_4868101
6_75sq_1371391216.jpg
2 https://igcdn-photos-f-a.akamaihd.net/hphotos-ak-xtp1/t51.2885-19/11111439_39590342725
6149_1369200645_a.jpg
3                              https://instagramimages-a.akamaihd.net/profiles/profile_25198603
0_75sq_1387005864.jpg
    full_name        id
1             48681016
2  Mertailor 369962997
3 Gio Pastori 251986030
> |
```

For the following code:

```
nrow(instaff)
```

The output is as follows:

```
[1] 429
```

Getting comments

We can get the comments posted on public media using the function `getComments`. This function will provide us with the recent comments posted on the specified media, and it can extract a maximum of 150 comments from a post. This function also extracts the details such as the text of the comments and details of the user who posted it, such as the name, ID, profile picture, and the comments ID. The code is as follows:

```
comm<- getComments("1027502496068994465_25025320", token)
```

The output is as follows:

```
150 comments
```

For the following code:

```
names(comm)
```

The output is as follows:

```
> names(comm)
[1] "created_time"      "text"                  "from_username"
[4] "from_id"           "from_profile_picture"  "from_full_name"
[7] "id"
>
```

In our example, we downloaded the most recent 150 comments, and all the details regarding the comments are stored in the data frame `comm`. Let's see what the snapshot of the output looks like using the following command:

```
tail(comm)
```

The output is as follows:

```
> tail(comm)
         created_time
145 2015-07-13 11:26:03
146 2015-07-13 11:28:40
147 2015-07-13 11:36:19
148 2015-07-13 11:37:40
149 2015-07-13 11:39:48
150 2015-07-13 11:41:09

text
145
Fo || <U+25CB> w4Fo || <U+25CB> w <ed><U+00A0><U+00BD><ed><U+00B0><U+00A4> / £ ik
€ s4 £ ik € s <ed><U+00A0><U+00BD><ed><U+00B1><U+008D>
146 <U+0644><U+0644><U+0625><U+0639><U+0644><U+0627><U+0646> <U+0641><U+064A> <U+
0645><U+062C><U+0645><U+0639> <U+0635><U+062D><U+0629> <U+0627><U+0644><U+0637><U
+0628><U+064A> <U+0628><U+0627><U+0644><U+0645><U+062F><U+064A><U+0646><U+0629> <
U+0627><U+0644><U+0645><U+0646><U+0648><U+0631><U+0629>   <U+0627><U+0644><U+0631>
<U+062C><U+0627><U+0621> <U+0627><U+0644><U+062A><U+0648><U+0627><U+0635><U+0644>
<U+0648><U+0627><U+062A><U+0633><U+0627><U+0628> <U+0660><U+0665><U+0660><U+0668>
<U+0661><U+0667><U+0666><U+0661><U+0667><U+0667>
147
@paulthompson I like it
148
Col
149
@instagram please stop deleting fan accounts. Too many have been deleted recently
and they have done nothing wrong, at all. They actually work for their followers
and it really makes them sad to see all their hard work & time get thrown away so
easily. Thank you.
150
Cool picture
        from_username    from_id
145         rizemania   33025362
146   seha_polyclinic 1386590280
147 moumitaswargiary 1145349660
148        sara_70003 1829928213
149    shawnmemendes 2093399411
150      bhaumik1611 1685725516
```

This is a rich source of text data that can be used for performing text analytics to understand the sentiments of the people. We will cover a few concepts of text processing later in this chapter.

Number of times hashtag is used

The function `getTagCount` helps us know the usage of the specified hashtag in the comments for the media post. We can use this function to get the occurrence of any hashtag. We will use this function to get the number of times the tags `greece` and `obama` are used:

```
Tag1<- getTagCount("greece", token)
Tag1
```

The output is as follows:

```
[1] 7805055
```

For `obama`:

```
Tag2<- getTagCount("obama", token)
Tag2
```

The output is as follows:

```
[1] 2416024
```

We can use this function to get the popularity of brands, users, and so on. We can also get trends by executing the function at a fixed time interval.

Exercise:

- Do a word cloud analysis on the recent comments posted in the account `Instagram`.
- Do an hourly trend analysis for a week on the number of times the following tags are used:
- `#love`
- `#instagood`
- `#me`
- `#tbt`
- `#followme`
- `#photooftheday`
- `#happy`
- `#tagforlikes`
- `#selfie`

For the preceding tags, get the following information:

- What are the top 3 tags that have the highest growth rate?
- Is there any daily seasonality in the preceding tags?
- What are the pairs of tags with highest similarity?
- This can be implemented by executing the function to capture the tag count on an hourly basis.
- Extract the pictures posted from the *New7wonders* of the world.

Building a dataset

In this section, we will create multiple datasets using a specific set of users as well as the hashtags that will be used for further analysis, so we can answer some interesting questions. We have created a list of popular users as well as some popular hashtags that are commonly used while sharing media related to travelling. All the users and the hashtags used for the analysis will be provided. The name of the CSV file is `UsersAndHashtags`, this CSV file will have two columns: one with the popular users and the other with the hashtags.

Place the aforementioned CSV file in the current working directory. You can get the current working directory using the function `getwd()`; alternatively, you can also change the working directory using the function `setwd()`. After placing the file in the current working directory, execute the following commands:

```
userAndTags<- read.csv("UsersAndHashtags.csv")
names(userAndTags)
head(userAndTags)
```

The output is as follows:

```
> head(userAndTags)
               Users       Hashtags
1            beyonce       monument
2  brooklynbeckham  worldheritage
3    charlizeafrica        amazing
4    prattprattpratt           trip
5       theellenshow   architecture
6         humansofny         travel
>
```

This is the list of celebrity profiles as well as travel-related hashtags that will help us extract important information.

User profile

First, we will get the complete profile information about these celebrity user profiles. We can get the profile information using the function `getUser`. We will loop through the preceding table to get the profile information about all the users. Since data extraction involves multiple API calls and, in some cases, might take more time, we will store the dataset in the local system using the function `write.csv`. In the following case, we have a counter on the number of users whose data has been processed so far; it will be printed on the screen. If the code breaks in between, it can be continued based on the counter. The code is as follows:

```
users<- userAndTags$Users
users<- as.matrix(users)
userprofiles = data.frame(matrix("", ncol = 8, nrow = 0))
for (i in 1:nrow(users))
{
   #uf<- getFollows(users[i,1], token)
usrp<- getUser(users[i,1], token)
userprofiles<- rbind(userprofiles, usrp)
print(i)

}
write.csv(userprofiles, "userprofiles.csv")
head(userprofiles, 3)
```

The output is as follows:

```
> head(userprofiles)
         username
1         beyonce
2 brooklynbeckham
3   charlizeafrica
4 prattprattpratt
5         popsugar
6       salmahayek

                                                                                         bio
1
2
3
4                     I use my twitter for jokes mostly. But I use my Instagram for deeper more meaningful stuff like pictures mostly.
5
6 After hundreds of impostors, years of procrastination, and a self-imposed allergy to technology, FINALLY I'm here. ¡Hola! This is truly Salma.
                    website
1     http://www.beyonce.com
2
3
4
5     http://www.popsugar.com
6 http://twitter.com/salmahayek
                                                                                 profile_picture
1         https://igcdn-photos-g-a.akamaihd.net/hphotos-ak-xft1/t51.2885-19/11098624_1632794343609174_1724291661_a.jpg
2 https://igcdn-photos-b-a.akamaihd.net/hphotos-ak-xpa1/t51.2885-19/s150x150/11191216_997536980258561_1248633090_a.jpg
3         https://igcdn-photos-h-a.akamaihd.net/hphotos-ak-xfa1/t51.2885-19/10175122_246931378828975_568099733_a.jpg
4         https://igcdn-photos-e-a.akamaihd.net/hphotos-ak-xpa1/t51.2885-19/10570060_731177430282340_844528433_a.jpg
5 https://igcdn-photos-c-a.akamaihd.net/hphotos-ak-xaf1/t51.2885-19/11410668_1623481421242586_1446105071_a.jpg
6         https://igcdn-photos-d-a.akamaihd.net/hphotos-ak-xap1/t51.2885-19/11078688_903536949669427_1338825742_a.jpg
        full_name media_count followed_by follows
1         Beyoncé        1068    39956644       0
2 Brooklyn Beckham          86     3563310     142
3   Charlize Theron          64      357358      37
4   prattprattpratt          70     1793147      27
5         POPSUGAR        4099      138978     689
6 Salma Hayek Pinault         70      192965     108
>
```

User media

Let's extract all the user-specific data. In order to do so, we need to get all the usernames and convert them into a matrix so that we can easily refer to the positions of the usernames. Then, we can create an empty data frame of the same dimensions as the produced output. The code is as follows:

```
users<- userAndTags$Users
users<- as.matrix(users)

usermedia <- data.frame(matrix("", ncol = 16, nrow = 0))
```

We are using a `for` loop to extract all the user data. In the following code, we are extracting just the 20 most recent posts from all the users using the function `getUserMedia`. We will keep appending the data to the existing dataset using the function `rbind`. The following code will not only produce a large dataset with the 20 most recent posts from all the users provided as input, but also download their media files to the folder named `users` in the current working directory. The code is as follows:

```
for (i in 7:nrow(users))
{
um<- getUserMedia(users[i,1], token, n=20, folder="users")
usermedia<- rbind(usermedia, um)
print(i)
}
head(usermedia)
```

The output is as follows:

```
> head(usermedia)
  X  type longitude latitude location_name location_id comments_count filter
1 1 image        NA       NA          <NA>          NA          13336 Normal
2 2 image        NA       NA          <NA>          NA           3570 Normal
3 3 image        NA       NA          <NA>          NA          10636 Normal
4 4 image        NA       NA          <NA>          NA           7542 Normal
5 5 image        NA       NA          <NA>          NA          12218   Aden
6 6 video        NA       NA          <NA>          NA          62584 Normal
         created_time                            link likes_count
1 2015-07-07 05:53:43 https://instagram.com/p/4OI8Lnvw2y/     998675
2 2015-07-06 06:20:24 https://instagram.com/p/4xnMw-vwyU/     598587
3 2015-07-06 06:03:42 https://instagram.com/p/4x1SVavw-u/    1190717
4 2015-07-06 02:40:02 https://instagram.com/p/4xN-o6vw_Z/    1186050
5 2015-07-03 06:43:50 https://instagram.com/p/4p7fwYPw_m/    1145703
6 2015-07-01 23:05:54 https://instagram.com/p/4miS2Mvw8L/    1257908
                                                                                                    image_url
1           https://scontent.cdninstagram.com/hphotos-xfa1/t51.2885-15/e15/11421839_1599743283614039_899889751_n.jpg
2  https://scontent.cdninstagram.com/hphotos-xaf1/t51.2885-15/s640x640/e35/sh0.08/11379007_942460589144554_912328289_n.jpg
3 https://scontent.cdninstagram.com/hphotos-xat1/t51.2885-15/s640x640/e35/sh0.08/10683799_944264715616129_2052940071_n.jpg
4  https://scontent.cdninstagram.com/hphotos-xaf1/t51.2885-15/s640x640/e35/sh0.08/11378179_123043894699043_637050024_n.jpg
5       https://scontent.cdninstagram.com/hphotos-xaf1/t51.2885-15/s640x640/e15/11374471_718666351594531_33970953_n.jpg
6           https://scontent.cdninstagram.com/hphotos-xfa1/t51.2885-15/e15/11379338_136176490047591_1254096861_n.jpg
                                caption username  user_id user_fullname
1                                  <NA>  beyonce 247944034       Beyoncé
2                                  <NA>  beyonce 247944034       Beyoncé
3                                 U.S.A  beyonce 247944034       Beyoncé
4 <ed><U+00A0><U+00BD><ed><U+00B2><U+008B>  beyonce 247944034       Beyoncé
5                                  <NA>  beyonce 247944034       Beyoncé
6 Never Too Late #LoveWins <U+2764><U+FE0F>  beyonce 247944034       Beyoncé
                        id
1 1023482335338630578_247944034
2 1022770991429782676_247944034
3 1022762578058612654_247944034
4 1022660069537288153_247944034
5 1020608457570455526_247944034
6 1019653194373861131_247944034
>
```

Travel-related media

After extracting the user data, we will now focus on the popular hashtags commonly used with regard to travel and sightseeing. The second column of the dataset provided has the list of hashtags. Similar to extracting the user data, we use the `for` loop to extract travel-related posts. In the following code, for each of the hashtags, we download 100 recent posts. Finally, we combine the data using the function `rbind`. The code is as follows:

```
tags<- userAndTags$Hashtags
tags<- as.matrix(tags)
for (i in 1:nrow(tags))
{
hm<- getUserMedia(tags[i,1], token, n=100, folder="tags")
hashmedia<- rbind(hashmedia, hm)
print(i)
}
head(hashmedia)
```

The output is as follows:

```
> head(hashmedia)
  x  type longitude latitude         location_name location_id comments_count
1 1 image        NA       NA                  <NA>          NA              0
2 2 image  21.00484 52.24965 Supreme Court Of Poland   274897269              0
3 3 image  21.01635 52.24837       Arkady Kubickiego      431186              0
4 4 image        NA       NA                  <NA>          NA              0
5 5 image  21.01426 52.24381    Anegdoty warszawskie   866051731              0
6 6 image  21.01340 52.23997 Sofitel Warsaw Victoria      554801              0
   filter      created_time                          link likes_count
1 Ludwig 2015-07-14 00:34:05 https://instagram.com/p/5Fl7JmJLVU/           1
2 Normal 2015-07-14 00:33:06 https://instagram.com/p/5FlOBnzHI8/           1
3 Normal 2015-07-14 00:29:37 https://instagram.com/p/5FlajdTHIV/           3
4   Rise 2015-07-14 00:27:42 https://instagram.com/p/5FlMdxysJP/           9
5 Normal 2015-07-14 00:26:38 https://instagram.com/p/5FlEm7THHr/           7
6 Normal 2015-07-14 00:24:06 https://instagram.com/p/5FkyHQzHHL/          12
                                                                       image_url
1       https://scontent.cdninstagram.com/hphotos-xaf1/t51.2885-15/e15/11358262_1345124968825553_1209888707_n.jpg
2 https://scontent.cdninstagram.com/hphotos-xfp1/t51.2885-15/s640x640/e35/sh0.08/927166_917176578368220_1125565774_n.jpg
3 https://scontent.cdninstagram.com/hphotos-xaf1/t51.2885-15/s640x640/e35/sh0.08/11419135_377134542479834_1287048671_n.jpg
4 https://scontent.cdninstagram.com/hphotos-xfa1/t51.2885-15/s640x640/e35/sh0.08/11313386_1631187377164427_140866725_n.jpg
5 https://scontent.cdninstagram.com/hphotos-xaf1/t51.2885-15/s640x640/e35/sh0.08/11351619_1025049187508263_1984030001_n.jpg
6 https://scontent.cdninstagram.com/hphotos-xfa1/t51.2885-15/s640x640/e35/sh0.08/11419070_833014000128720_1140642529_n.jpg

caption
1
igueldeallende #mexicomagico #mexicolindo #ig_mexico #worldheritage
2                                    Court House in warsaw. #warsaw #warszawa #130715 #instaw
urthouse #design #architecture #unesco #worldheritage #trees #grass
3                           old house in warsaw. #warsaw #warszawa #130715 #instawarsaw #iphone6plus #oldtown #unesco #w
eau #architecture #design #facade #poland #summer #door #woodendoor
4                       St. Sophia Cathedral \n#Kiev #ukraine #explore #travel #cathedral #StSophia #StSophiaCathedral
icanabroad #igtravel #beauty #architecture #love #worldheritagelist
5                          Statue in Old Town warsaw. #warsaw #warszawa #130715 #instawarsaw #iphone6plus #poland #art #s
unesco #worldheritage #park #garden #flowers #trees #clouds #summer
6 Yellow grass... warsaw needs more than one rain shower! #warsaw #warszawa #130715 #instawarsaw #iphone6plus #grass #architectu
ds #unesco #worldheritage #poland #summer #artdeco #artnouveau #art
     username    user_id        user_fullname
1     soviore 1783287348 Marinelly Diaz Saporiti
```

Since the user data as well as the hashtag data are similar to each other, we combine the datasets to produce a common dataset that could be used for the analysis. The code is as follows:

```
alldata<- rbind(usermedia, hashmedia)
head(alldata)
```

Who do they follow?

In addition to the preceding datasets, we will also create a dataset on whom the celebrity users follow on Instagram. This information will be very useful to provide recommendations to various celebrity users whom they would like to follow based on similar user behavior. We will be discussing these recommendations in detail later in this chapter.

We will use the following code to read the list of users from our dataset userAndTags and convert them to matrix format using the function as.matrix and finally use a for loop on the users to extract basic details of the accounts they follow.

```
users<- userAndTags$Users
users<- as.matrix(users)
userfollows = data.frame(matrix("", ncol = 7, nrow = 0))
for (i in 1:nrow(users))
{
uf<- getFollows(users[i,1], token)
auf<- cbind(users[i,1], uf)
userfollows<- rbind(userfollows, auf)
print(i)

}
nrow(userfollows)
write.csv(userfollows, "userfollows.csv")
head(userfollows)
```

 Note that the for loop in the preceding code will break if any of the users have zero follows. Hence we have the counter in place, so that we can change the starting pointer in the for loop, and continue to pull the data until the list is completed.

The output is as follows:

```
> head(userfollows)
    X     users.i..1.        username bio website
1 1 brooklynbeckham          uwheels  NA      NA
2 2 brooklynbeckham ashleycharles14   NA      NA
3 3 brooklynbeckham   jorelljohnson   NA      NA
4 4 brooklynbeckham       max_makaka  NA      NA
5 5 brooklynbeckham      beezymason   NA      NA
6 6 brooklynbeckham nathangartside5   NA      NA
                                                                                           profile_picture
1            https://igcdn-photos-a-a.akamaihd.net/hphotos-ak-xfa1/t51.2885-19/11357945_1128703060488056_218082261_a.jpg
2            https://igcdn-photos-a-a.akamaihd.net/hphotos-ak-xpf1/t51.2885-19/11015560_793747430717560_2077439940_a.jpg
3            https://igcdn-photos-e-a.akamaihd.net/hphotos-ak-xpf1/t51.2885-19/10731578_732482456846260_1214795391_a.jpg
4 https://igcdn-photos-f-a.akamaihd.net/hphotos-ak-xaf1/t51.2885-19/s150x150/11419108_1606266189643405_516880645_a.jpg
5            https://igcdn-photos-e-a.akamaihd.net/hphotos-ak-xpf1/t51.2885-19/11117015_616439008493772_115272205_a.jpg
6            https://igcdn-photos-e-a.akamaihd.net/hphotos-ak-xat1/t51.2885-19/11055894_949534028420108_1355003259_a.jpg
                                                                            full_name
1                                                                             U wheels
2                                                                       Ashley Charles
3                                                                       Jorell Johnson
4 Makaka 8 <U+26BD><ed><U+00A0><U+00BD><ed><U+00B2><U+00AF><ed><U+00A0><U+00BC><ed><U+00BC><U+009F>
5                                                                        Brandon Mason
6                                                                       Nathan Gartside
          id
1 2015755375
2  758768642
3  699548027
4 1271798036
5  328411188
6 1077726241
> |
```

Thus the preceding dataset has the celebrity username followed by the users they follow, along with their basic profile details. For the recommendation engine, the first two columns will be sufficient. We will be using this dataset for further analysis.

Popular personalities

From the dataset we built, we will work on identifying the most popular users using different aspects. Let's see those in detail.

Who has the most followers?

We can get the users with most number of followers from the dataset `userprofiles` by sorting the data using the column `followed_by` and using the function `order`. The following code will return the dataset by sorting the data in the descending order based on the column `followed_by`. The code is as follows:

```
mostfollowed<- userprofiles[with(userprofiles,
order(-followed_by)), ]
head(mostfollowed$full_name, 15)
```

The output is as follows:

```
> head(mostfollowed$full_name, 15)
 [1] "Beyoncé"             "Kim Kardashian West" "Selena Gomez"
 [4] "Khloé"               "Miley Cyrus"         "Cristiano Ronaldo"
 [7] "Jennifer Lopez"      "Leo Messi"           "therock"
[10] "Kourtney Kardashian" "nike"                "Cara Delevingne"
[13] "Justin Timberlake"   "Shakira"             "champagnepapi"
>
```

Who follows more people?

To know the user who follows the most number of people, we use the same dataset `userprofiles`. Everything is similar to the previous one, but we need to use the column `follows` instead of `followed_by`. The code is as follows:

```
mostfollows<- userprofiles[with(userprofiles, order(-follows)), ]
head(mostfollows$full_name, 15)
```

The output is as follows:

```
> head(mostfollows$full_name, 15)
 [1] "Cara Delevingne" "Jesse Williams"    "Emma Roberts"  "J O E  J O N A S"
 [5] "Jaime King"      "Jessica Alba"      "champagnepapi" "Jennifer Lopez"
 [9] "Puff Daddy"      ""                  "Joy Bryant"    "Lena Dunham"
[13] "POPSUGAR"        "Candice Swanepoel" "Minka Kelly"
>
```

The preceding output shows the users who follow the most number of people on Instagram.

Who shared most media?

Now, let's see who are the most active users and who have shared the most number of pictures/videos on Instagram. We use the dataset `userprofiles`:

```
mostmedia <- userprofiles[with(userprofiles,
order(-media_count)), ]
head(mostmedia$full_name, 15)
```

The output is as follows:

```
> head(mostmedias$full_name, 15)
 [1] "Puff Daddy"    "POPSUGAR"            "Miley Cyrus"
 [4] "James Franco"  "Kim Kardashian West" "Ashley Benson"
 [7] "Khloé"         "Cara Delevingne"     "Mindy Kaling"
[10] "Emmy Rossum"   ""                    "Lucy Hale"
[13] "Jessica Alba"  "champagnepapi"       "Mena.\xed��\xed��"
>
```

Overall top users

So far, we have explored the popular users based on the factors `followed_by`, `follows`, and `media_count` from the dataset `userprofiles`. In the following code, we will get the overall active users by using all of the aforementioned factors. The code is as follows:

```
userprofiles$overallmetric<-
((userprofiles$media_count/max(userprofiles$media_count)) +
(userprofiles$followed_by/max(userprofiles$followed_by))
+(userprofiles$followed_by/max(userprofiles$followed_by)))*100
```

In the preceding code, we normalize the values of each of the factors to the range of 0-100. Then, we add them up to come up with the final score. The final score can have a maximum value of 300. The code is as follows:

```
overallmet<- userprofiles[with(userprofiles,
order(-overallmetric)), ]
head(overallmet$full_name, 15)
```

The output is as follows:

```
> head(overallmet$full_name, 15)
 [1] "Kim Kardashian West" "Beyoncé"            "Selena Gomez"
 [4] "Miley Cyrus"         "Khloé"              "Jennifer Lopez"
 [7] "Kourtney Kardashian" "Puff Daddy"         "Cristiano Ronaldo"
[10] "therock"             "Cara Delevingne"    "Leo Messi"
[13] "nike"                "champagnepapi"      "Ashley Benson"
>
```

These are the most active users based on all of the previously mentioned factors. These are the various analyses to get us the most popular users on Instagram.

Most viral media

We can find out about the media which went most viral. To get that information, we will use the dataset `alldata`, and the columns `comments_count` and `likes_count`. The following code will help us to identify the media that had the most number of comments as well as the one with the most number of likes:

```
mostcomm<- alldata[with(alldata, order(-comments_count)), ]
head(mostcomm, 1)
```

The output is as follows:

```
> head(mostcomm, 1)
        X  type longitude latitude location_name location_id comments_count filter
1613 1613 image        NA       NA         <NA>          NA          84137 Normal
            created_time                                 link likes_count
1613 2015-06-25 06:35:31 https://instagram.com/p/4VULv6PM2K/      1542382

image_url
1613 https://scontent.cdninstagram.com/hphotos-xaf1/t51.2885-15/e15/11378271_144942091535
9014_2086564367_n.jpg
     caption username    user_id user_fullname                               id
1613    <NA> leomessi 427553890      Leo Messi 10148806059329310090_427553890
>
```

We can get the media post with the maximum number of likes by sorting the content in descending order based on the column `likes_count` using the function `order`. This can be implemented using the following code:

```
mostlikes<- alldata[with(alldata, order(-likes_count)), ]
head(mostlikes, 1)
```

The output is as follows:

```
> head(mostlikes, 1)
        X  type longitude latitude location_name location_id comments_count filter
1619 1619 image        NA       NA         <NA>          NA          37710 Normal
            created_time                                 link likes_count
1619 2015-06-07 03:18:40 https://instagram.com/p/3mnWQqvMx8/      1911646

image_url
1619 https://scontent.cdninstagram.com/hphotos-xaf1/t51.2885-15/e15/11358981_144507450579
4826_49119342_n.jpg
                                     caption username    user_id user_fullname
1619 Campeonesssssss !!!!!!!!!! Vamossss carajooooo leomessi 427553890      Leo Messi
                                  id
1619 1001661020675820668_427553890
>
```

Finding the most popular destination

We explored some of the user metrics as well as the media metrics. Now, we will explore the geography of the media posts. We can get the geo-location if it has been enabled by the user. We will perform this analysis on the dataset `alldata`.

Locations

In the following code, we are just getting the unique locations found in the dataset collected by us. Since we are getting the data with the help of a query, we need to load the `sqldf` package in the R console and use the function `na.omit` to remove the posts without any location details. The following code consolidates the locations and finally, using the function `nrow`, we get to know about the unique number of locations from where the posts were made.

```
library(sqldf)
names(alldata)
allloc<- sqldf("select distinct location_name from alldata")
allloc<- na.omit(allloc)
nrow(allloc)
```

The output is as follows:

```
[1] 432
```

There are posts from 432 different location in the dataset collected by us. Let's get a snapshot of some of the locations:

```
head(allloc, 20)
```

The output is as follows:

```
> head(allloc, 20)
                       location_name
2                Cannes Film Festival
3                 STONE ROSE NEW YORK
4                       Shubert Alley
5                      The Jane Hotel
6          Belasco Theater on Broadway
7                          jane hotel
8                                 USA
9              Ancient City Of Pompei
10                San Domenico Palace
11                    Siracusa Sicily
12                      Savoca Sicily
13                  Runyon Canyon Park
14                     Grand Park Wuxi
15         Mýkonos, Kikladhes, Greece
16                Soho House Istanbul
17                   Istanbul -Turkey
18 Dolmabache, Istanbul, Turkey
19                      Topaki Palace
20          Belasco Theatre New York
21                      The Town Hall
> |
```

Locations with most likes

We have seen all the locations from where the posts were made. Now, we will see which location, the posts with the maximum number of likes were made from. We can get this data by using the `group by` function in SQL, and then sorting the data based on the descending order of the total likes received. The code is as follows:

```
loclikes<- sqldf("select location_name, sum(likes_count) as
totlikes from alldata group by location_name")
loc<- loclikes[with(loclikes, order(-totlikes)), ]
loc<- na.omit(loc)
head(loc, 25)
```

The output is as follows:

```
> head(loc, 25)
                         location_name totlikes
343            Stockholm Archipelago   451732
426                       jane hotel   451014
387                      Tower Bridge   436846
55                   Berlin, Germany   434332
92            Chula Vista, California   426811
44                  Barceloneta Beach   423563
124                  Epsom View Point   396870
211                       London SW19   337544
386                   Toronto, Canada   334469
413                Winnipeg, Manitoba   332008
320                     Shubert Alley   263100
323                    Siracusa Sicily   199881
393                               USA   180262
36              Ancient City Of Pompei   131510
314                     Savoca Sicily   118466
302                STONE ROSE NEW YORK   110579
377        The White House South Lawn   106300
368                    The Jane Hotel    74637
177                   Istanbul -Turkey    71800
50         Belasco Theater on Broadway    60848
306               San Domenico Palace    38798
376    The white House Kitchen Garden    37264
233         Mýkonos, Kikladhes, Greece    37202
51          Belasco Theatre New York    29072
333                Soho House Istanbul    27230
>
```

Locations most talked about

We assume the total comments made in the post as a proxy for the location most talked about, though the comments might not really be about the place. This can be implemented in a way similar to the likes for a location by using the column `comments_count` instead of `likes_count`. The code is as follows:

```
loccomments<- sqldf("select location_name, sum(comments_count) as
totcomm from alldata group by location_name")
loccomm<- loccomments[with(loccomments, order(-totcomm)), ]
loccomm<- na.omit(loccomm)
```

The following output shows us the locations that had posts that were most talked about compared to others. We can see that the location with most likes is quite different from the location with most comments:

```
head(loccomm, 15)
```

The output is as follows:

```
> head(loccomm, 15)
                  location_name totcomm
314              Savoca Sicily    2630
323             Siracusa Sicily    2408
92       Chula Vista, California    2305
36       Ancient City Of Pompei    1882
44             Barceloneta Beach    1746
377 The White House South Lawn    1627
55               Berlin, Germany    1620
343        Stockholm Archipelago    1555
426                  jane hotel    1497
320               Shubert Alley    1480
124            Epsom View Point    1446
387                Tower Bridge    1370
393                         USA    1250
211               London SW19    1183
413          Winnipeg, Manitoba    1002
>
```

What are people saying about these locations?

Having seen some of the quantitative measure of the locations, we will now see what people are saying about those locations, or in those posts made by them. For this analysis, we use the text and tags found under the caption. After collecting all the caption text, we perform the text analysis.

To perform text analysis, we need to load some packages that enable text analysis. For this section, we need to load the package wordcloud for plotting the word cloud and tm to perform some processing on the text data and make it usable for the text analysis. The code is as follows:

```
library(wordcloud)
library(tm)
```

We first break the sentences into words using the function strsplit. Then, we perform a series of steps to remove the special characters from the dataset, convert them into lower case words, and finally remove the standard stop words. The code is as follows:

```
words<- strsplit(as.character(alldata$caption), " ")
```

```
words<- lapply(words, function(x) x[grep("^[A-Za-z0-9]+$", x)])
words<- unlist(words)
words<- tolower(words)
#Remove stop words
stopWords<- stopwords("en")
"%!in%" <- function(x,table) match(x,table, nomatch = 0) == 0
words<- words[words %!in% stopWords]
```

The function `table` creates a frequency on the number of times a certain word occurs. Using the function `wordcloud`, we plot the plot the word cloud. We pass some parameters, such as the color range for the text, to the function `wordcloud` and we plot only the words that had more than 20 occurrences. The code is as follows:

```
allwords<- as.data.frame(table(words))
wordcloud(allwords$words, allwords$Freq, random.order = FALSE,
min.freq=20, colors = brewer.pal(2, "Dark2"))
```

The output is as follows:

Most repeating locations

Having seen some of the metrics on location, we will now look at the repetition of posts made from a particular location. The following query will get us the required information and sort the locations that were repeated the most. Since the dataset used in our case is not huge, it is possible that a location could have come out on top because of repeated posts from a single user. The code is as follows:

```
locations<- sqldf("select location_name, count(location_id) as
locid from alldata group by location_name")
```

```
location<- locations[with(locations, order(-locid)), ]
location<- na.omit(location)
head(location,5)
```

The output is as follows:

location_name	locid
Stonehenge	8
Dunston Staithes	5
Shubert Alley	4
Sibenska Katedrala	4

Exercise:

We have found some really interesting metrics that can be measured based on an Instagram post. Here are some more metrics that you can try:

- Which captions (hashtags) have the tendency to increase the likes?
- Which user's post has generated more likes as well as comments?
- Identify some new metrics for the geo-location and compute it using R.

Clustering the pictures

Clustering is an example of unsupervised learning as there is no prior knowledge of the groups present in the dataset. It is a method of dividing the dataset into different groups based on various parameters of the dataset. Each group is called a cluster, and the various objects present in a group will be share some similarities as well as dissimilarities when compared with the objects outside the group. We will cover the clustering algorithm in this section.

One of the greatest examples of the clustering algorithm would be the search engine; where the pages that are closely related to each other are shown together, and the pages that are different are kept away as far as possible. The most important factor here is the factor that we consider to measure the similarity or the dissimilarity between the objects.

In order to implement the clustering algorithms in R, we need to load the package fpc into the R environment. The package fpc, a flexible procedure for clustering, has multiple functions to implement various kinds of clustering techniques. The code is as follows:

```
library(fpc)
data<- alldata
cdata<- subset(data, select= c(type, comments_count,
likes_count, filter)
```

We will use the `alldata` dataset and select only a few numerical and categorical columns for performing the clustering analysis. After selecting the desired columns from the dataset, we convert the categorical columns to the integer format. Standard clustering algorithm can't be applied on the categorical data because the Euclidian distance function isn't meaningful on discrete values. By executing the following code, we also get to know the number of characters present in the column `caption` using the function `nchar`.

```
colnames(cdata) <- c("type","comments","likes","filter")
cdata$filter<- as.integer(cdata$filter)
cdata$type<- as.integer(cdata$type)
cdata$lencap<- nchar(as.character(data$caption))
head(cdata)
```

In the preceding code, for the purpose of learning, we are converting the categorical data into integer, as the clustering algorithm works for integer data. It is generally not preferred to do so. Also, it is advisable to scale the numerical columns to standardize the values so as to give equal weights to them.

The output is as follows:

```
> head(cdata)
  type comments   likes filter lencap
1    1    13336  998675     25      2
2    1     3570  598587     25      2
3    1    10636 1190717     25      5
4    1     7542 1186050     25     40
5    1    12218 1145703      2      2
6    2    62584 1257908     25     41
>
```

The preceding dataset is the one we will use for clustering analysis. Before performing clustering analysis, it is good to identify the ideal number of clusters based on the patterns in the data. We can identify the ideal number of cluster by two different methods. Let's explore each one of them. First, we identify the ideal number of clusters using the function `pamk`. This calls the function `pam` or `clara` to perform partitioning around the medoids clustering with the number of clusters estimated by optimum average silhouette width. The code is as follows:

```
clusters<- pamk(cdata)
n<-clusters$nc
```

This preceding function is computationally intensive so might take a very long time for even a slightly larger dataset. Hence, we will also cover a manual method to identify the ideal number of clusters. The code is as follows:

```
# Code from Tal Galili's post based on Kabacoff's book - http://www.r-
statistics.com/2013/08/k-means-clustering-from-r-in-action/
cdata<- data
wss<- (nrow(cdata)-1)*sum(apply(cdata,2,var))
for (i in 2:25) wss[i] <- sum(kmeans(cdata,
centers=i)$withinss)
plot(1:25, wss, type="b", xlab="Number of Clusters",
ylab="Within groups sum of squares")
```

The preceding code is taken from Tal Galili's post based on Kabacoff's book. It generates the following output and we need to read the graph to arrive at the ideal number of clusters. Logically, as the number of clusters increase, the sum of squared errors reduce. If there are *n* objects in a dataset then *n* clusters would result in 0 error, but ideally we need to stop at some point. As per the theories, the rate of decrease in the sum of errors will drop suddenly at a point and that should be considered as the ideal number of clusters. According to the following graph, the ideal number of cluster is 4.

The output is as follows:

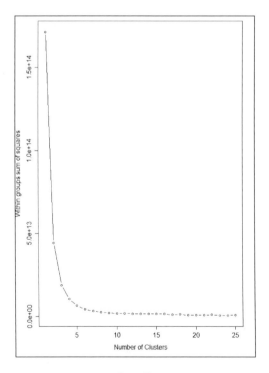

As per our observations, the ideal number of clusters should be 4. Hence, we will go ahead and implement the clustering algorithm with 4 clusters. We build the clusters using the function `kmeans`. We get the number of objects in each cluster using the function `table`. We can also perform the aggregation of the objects within the same group using the function `aggregate`. We can also plot cluster output using the function `plotcluster`. The code is as follows

```
fit<- kmeans(cdata, 4)
table(fit$cluster)
```

Here are the number of elements present in each of the clusters:

```
> table(fit$cluster)

   1    2    3    4
3160   43  105  262
>
```

We use the function `aggregate` to get the mean value of the objects in each of the groups for the various columns.

```
aggregate(cdata,by=list(fit$cluster),FUN=mean)
```

The output is as follows:

```
> aggregate(cdata,by=list(fit$cluster),FUN=mean)
  Group.1      type   comments        likes   filter    lencap
1       1 1.052848   263.7611     17051.44 23.34367 253.10791
2       2 1.023256 26602.2326 1410549.44 24.04651  89.60465
3       3 1.076190  8153.6857   805484.98 24.70476 109.52381
4       4 1.087786  3704.9771   334015.77 24.42748 120.81298
>
```

From the preceding output, we get a better understanding about the dataset, such as the average value of various attributes in different clusters. Since the objects in a cluster exhibit a similar behavior, the clusters can be considered for different experiments. The code is as follows:

```
plotcluster(cdata, fit$cluster)
```

The output is as follows:

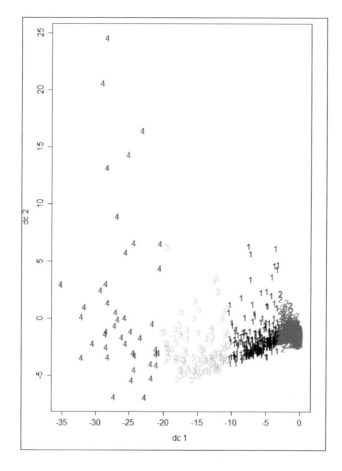

The preceding output gives us the pictorial representation of the number of clusters based on the principal components of the variables in the dataset; with the color coding, it becomes easy to see the clusters.

Some of the problems that can be solved through the implementation of a clustering algorithm are as follows:

- In the medical field, it can be used to predict the likelihood of a disease
- It can be used for matching DNA to a suitable group
- It can be used for grouping similar customers for marketing campaigns

- For academics, it can be used to group students based on their similarity of their various fields of research

Exercise:

Consider a dataset with only numerical values and implement the clustering algorithm by identifying the ideal number of clusters using the manual method as well as using the function. Also, try to implement the other clustering algorithm and check how the results vary.

Converting a categorical value into integer values is not advisable in any real world problem. In this case, we have performed this for ease of understanding.

Recommendations to the users

Recommendation has become very common nowadays. Many online companies like Amazon, Facebook, LinkedIn, and so on provide recommendations. These recommendations are produced by the recommendation system that is nothing but an algorithm that uses some of the historic data to predict what the user would like. The recommendation can be implemented using the collaborative filtering algorithm, which can be implemented using either user-based or item-based methodology. In this section, we will see in detail the implementation of the algorithm using user-based filtering.

How to do it

We will use the information of the users whose details we have downloaded, and the users whom they follow, and we will build the recommendation engine based on this data. Since we have already downloaded the data, we will read the data using the function `read.csv`:

```
userfollows<- read.csv("userfollows.csv")
names(userfollows)
```

The output is as follows:

```
> names(userfollows)
[1] "X"                "users.i..1."     "username"       "bio"
[5] "website"          "profile_picture" "full_name"      "id"
>
```

We have the preceding variable in the dataset. In order to build the recommendation engine and provide recommendations to the users, we would just need two columns. Hence, we select those two columns using the function `data.frame`:

```
fdata<- data.frame(userfollows$users.i..1., userfollows$username)
colnames(fdata) <- c("user","follows")
head(fdata)
```

The output is as follows:

```
> head(fdata)
              user          follows
1 brooklynbeckham          uwheels
2 brooklynbeckham ashleycharles14
3 brooklynbeckham    jorelljohnson
4 brooklynbeckham      max_makaka
5 brooklynbeckham      beezymason
6 brooklynbeckham nathangartside5
> |
```

Now, we have to pivot the dataset in such a way that the users become the column axis and the users whom they follow, as the rows. So, it becomes easy for us to compute the correlation between the users. In order to pivot the data, we need to use the function `dcast.data.table`, which requires the package `data.table`. The following code will pivot the raw dataset:

```
library(data.table)
pivoting<- data.table(fdata)
pivotdata<-dcast.data.table(pivoting,
follows ~ user, fun.aggregate=length, value.var="user")
write.csv(pivotdata, "pivot-follows.csv")
```

The preceding pivot function might be slightly time consuming depending on the size of the actual dataset, and it is better to write the converted file in to the local system so that it can be reused. Let's see what the pivoted dataset would look like:

```
data<-read.csv("pivot-follows.csv")
colnames(data)
head(data)
```

The output is as follows:

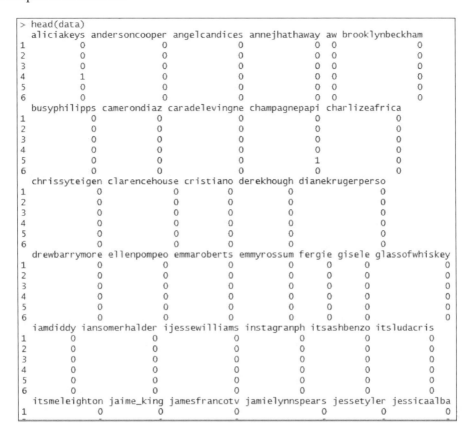

```
> head(data)
  aliciakeys andersoncooper angelcandices annejhathaway aw brooklynbeckham
1          0              0             0             0  0                0
2          0              0             0             0  0                0
3          0              0             0             0  0                0
4          1              0             0             0  0                0
5          0              0             0             0  0                0
6          0              0             0             0  0                0
  busyphilipps camerondiaz caradelevingne champagnepapi charlizeafrica
1            0           0              0             0              0
2            0           0              0             0              0
3            0           0              0             0              0
4            0           0              0             0              0
5            0           0              0             1              0
6            0           0              0             0              0
  chrissyteigen clarencehouse cristiano derekhough dianekrugerperso
1             0             0         0          0                0
2             0             0         0          0                0
3             0             0         0          0                0
4             0             0         0          0                0
5             0             0         0          0                0
6             0             0         0          0                0
  drewbarrymore ellenpompeo emmaroberts emmyrossum fergie gisele glassofwhiskey
1             0           0           0          0      0      0             0
2             0           0           0          0      0      0             0
3             0           0           0          0      0      0             0
4             0           0           0          0      0      0             0
5             0           0           0          0      0      0             0
6             0           0           0          0      0      0             0
  iamdiddy iansomerhalder ijessewilliams instagranph itsashbenzo itsludacris
1        0              0              0          0           0           0
2        0              0              0          0           0           0
3        0              0              0          0           0           0
4        0              0              0          0           0           0
5        0              0              0          0           0           0
6        0              0              0          0           0           0
  itsmeleighton jaime_king jamesfrancotv jamielynnspears jessetyler jessicaalba
1             0          0             0               0          0           0
```

 The preceding screenshot is just a part of the output.

After writing the file to the system, we need to remove the first two columns which are not required for building the recommendations. This can either be done manually; by deleting from the Excel file, or by using the following code:

```
data.ubs<- (data[,!(names(data) %in% c("users"))])
```

We can compute the similarity of the users using different methods. In our case, we will use the cosine similarity technique to get the similarity score for all the user pairs. In our dataset, zero means that the user is not following. If we consider those rows with zero, while computing the similarity using correlation or any other technique, we will end up with a biased output that is far from reality. Hence, while computing the similarity score, we will consider only the nonzero rows. The following function computes the similarity between the users using the cosine similarity method .Other methods that could be used are Pearson correlation similarity and by also counting the co-occurrence:

```
getCosine<- function(x,y)
{
dat<- cbind(x,y)
   #f<- as.matrix(dat)
f<- as.data.frame(dat)
   # Remove the rows with zeros
datn<- f[-which(rowSums(f==0)>0),]
if(nrow(datn) > 2)
   {
this.cosine<- sum(x*y) / (sqrt(sum(x*x)) * sqrt(sum(y*y)))
   }
else
   {
this.cosine<- 0
   }
return(this.cosine)
}
```

Now, we need to build a similarity matrix that will tell us how similar the users are to each other. Before computing the similarity, we will build an empty matrix that can be used to store the similarity:

```
data.ubs.similarity<- matrix(NA,
nrow=ncol(data.ubs),ncol=ncol(data.ubs),dimnames=list(colnames(
data.ubs),colnames(data.ubs)))
```

We can now start replacing the empty cells in the similarity matrix with the actual similarity score. In case of the cosine similarity, the range will be from -1 to +1. The following loop will help in computing the similarity between all the users. If there isn't enough data to compute the similarity as per our function, it will return zero. The print statement in the following loop will help us understand the progress of the loop. Depending on the dataset, the time taken would vary. In general, `for` loops are time consuming. The code is as follows:

```
for(i in 1:ncol(data.ubs)) {
```

```
    # Loop through the columns for each column
for(j in 1:ncol(data.ubs)) {
    # Fill in placeholder with cosine similarities
data.ubs.similarity[i,j] <- getCosine(as.matrix(data.ubs[i]),as.
matrix(data.ubs[j]))
    }
print(i)
}
# Back to dataframe - Similarity matrix
data.ubs.similarity<- as.data.frame(data.ubs.similarity)
head(data.ubs.similarity)
```

We get the following output:

```
> head(data.ubs.similarity)
                aliciakeys andersoncooper angelcandices annejhathaway
aliciakeys      1.00000000     0.02102586    0.03937543             0
andersoncooper  0.02102586     1.00000000    0.02092753             0
angelcandices   0.03937543     0.02092753    1.00000000             0
annejhathaway   0.00000000     0.00000000    0.00000000             1
aw              0.02175713     0.00000000    0.03867033             0
brooklynbeckham 0.01396482     0.00000000    0.03309408             0
                        aw brooklynbeckham busyphilipps camerondiaz
aliciakeys      0.02175713      0.01396482   0.03357711   0.0000000
andersoncooper  0.00000000      0.00000000   0.01147230   0.0000000
angelcandices   0.03867033      0.03309408   0.01392503   0.0000000
annejhathaway   0.00000000      0.00000000   0.00000000   0.0000000
aw              1.00000000      0.04114425   0.07419563   0.0555937
brooklynbeckham 0.04114425      1.00000000   0.02539866   0.0000000
                caradelevingne champagnepapi charlizeafrica chrissyteigen
aliciakeys         0.061420459    0.04711529     0.02735765    0.03357134
andersoncooper     0.008394215    0.00000000     0.00000000    0.00000000
angelcandices      0.115716456    0.01545987     0.00000000    0.07019821
annejhathaway      0.000000000    0.00000000     0.00000000    0.00000000
aw                 0.057002955    0.02242392     0.04836194    0.05236439
brooklynbeckham    0.060398189    0.04660526     0.00000000    0.03883834
                clarencehouse cristiano derekhough dianekrugerperso
aliciakeys         0.03144855         0 0.02496346       0.02564103
andersoncooper     0.00000000         0 0.00000000       0.00000000
angelcandices      0.00000000         0 0.00000000       0.09114683
annejhathaway      0.00000000         0 0.00000000       0.00000000
aw                 0.00000000         0 0.00000000       0.06345830
brooklynbeckham    0.00000000         0 0.00000000       0.00000000
                drewbarrymore ellenpompeo emmaroberts emmyrossum     fergie
aliciakeys         0.02441931  0.07775528  0.03245785 0.01109400 0.01677256
andersoncooper     0.00000000  0.02277142  0.01901122 0.02526993 0.00000000
```

 The preceding screenshot is just a part of the output.

Thus, the data frame `data.ubs.similarity` will hold the actual similarity between the users. After getting the similarity matrix, we need to get the top 10 neighbors for each user.

The code is as follows:

```
# Get the top 10 neighbours for each
data.neighbours<- matrix(NA, nrow=ncol(data.ubs.similarity),ncol=11,di
mnames=list(colnames(data.ubs.similarity)))
for(i in 1:ncol(data.ubs))
{
   # Setting threshold for avoiding zeros
n<- length(data.ubs.similarity[,i])
thres<- sort(data.ubs.similarity[,i],partial=n-10)[n-10]
if(thres> 0.020)
    {
      # Choosing the top 10 recommendations
data.neighbours[i,] <- (t(head(n=11,rownames(data.ubs.
similarity[order(data.ubs.similarity[,i],decreasing=TRUE),][i])))))
    }
else
    {
data.neighbours[i,] <- ""
    }
}
```

In the preceding code, we take up one user at a time and then sort the similarity score of the user with all the other users such that the pair with highest similarity comes first. Then, we stop by just filtering the first 10 for each of the users. This is recommended for us. We can see the recommendations given for a few users using the following code:

```
head(data.neighbours)
```

The output is as follows:

```
> head(data.neighbours)
                     [,1]                  [,2]                  [,3]
aliciakeys           "aliciakeys"          "johnlegend"          "ijessewilliams"
andersoncooper       ""                    ""                    ""
angelcandices        "angelcandices"       "caradelevingne"      "krisjenner"
annejhathaway        ""                    ""                    ""
aw                   "aw"                  "mindykaling"         "lenadunham"
brooklynbeckham      "brooklynbeckham"     "itsashbenzo"         "khloekardashian"
                     [,4]                  [,5]                  [,6]
aliciakeys           "ellenpompeo"         "randyjackson"        "krisjenner"
andersoncooper       ""                    ""                    ""
angelcandices        "gisele"              "dianekrugerperso"    "jaime_king"
annejhathaway        ""                    ""                    ""
aw                   "reesewitherspoon"    "popsugar"            "msleamichele"
brooklynbeckham      "krisjenner"          "popsugar"            "randyjackson"
                     [,7]                  [,8]                  [,9]
aliciakeys           "popsugar"            "iamdiddy"            "khloekardashian"
andersoncooper       ""                    ""                    ""
angelcandices        "itsashbenzo"         "emmaroberts"         "mileycyrus"
annejhathaway        ""                    ""                    ""
aw                   "itsashbenzo"         "emmaroberts"         "busyphilipps"
brooklynbeckham      "kimkardashian"       "caradelevingne"     "emmaroberts"
                     [,10]                 [,11]
aliciakeys           "caradelevingne"      "kimkardashian"
andersoncooper       ""                    ""
angelcandices        "jessicaalba"         "ellenpompeo"
annejhathaway        ""                    ""
aw                   "minkak"              "ellenpompeo"
brooklynbeckham      "msleamichele"        "leomessi"
> |
```

 The preceding screenshot is just a part of the output.

Top three recommendations

In the preceding recommendation list, we find that the first recommendation is the same as that of the original user. This is mostly because of the self-similarity computation and it has to be removed. The preceding data frame view is not very clear, so there is an Excel view below, where the first column is the celebrity users, who are the subject of our analysis, and the next three columns are the users who are similar to them. Here are some of the celebrity users and their top three similar users.

Celebrity Users	Recommendation1	Recommendation2	Recommendation3
aliciakeys	johnlegend	ijessewilliams	ellenpompeo
angelcandices	caradelevingne	krisjenner	gisele
aw	mindykaling	lenadunham	reesewitherspoon
brooklynbeckham	itsashbenzo	khloekardashian	krisjenner
busyphilipps	mindykaling	lenadunham	reesewitherspoon
camerondiaz	reesewitherspoon	msleamichele	mindykaling
caradelevingne	angelcandices	popsugar	emmaroberts
champagnepapi	iamdiddy	ijessewilliams	khloekardashian
charlizeafrica	randyjackson	ellenpompeo	aw
chrissyteigen	johnlegend	khloekardashian	popsugar
derekhough	juleshough	glassofwhiskey	msleamichele
dianekrugerperso	katebosworth	jaime_king	reesewitherspoon
drewbarrymore	reesewitherspoon	minkak	jaime_king
ellenpompeo	reesewitherspoon	jessicaalba	minkak
emmaroberts	itsashbenzo	jaime_king	jessicaalba
emmyrossum	jessicaalba	jaime_king	reesewitherspoon
fergie	joshduhamel	mileycyrus	popsugar
gisele	angelcandices	ellenpompeo	jaime_king
glassofwhiskey	juleshough	msleamichele	emmaroberts
iamdiddy	champagnepapi	ijessewilliams	randyjackson
iansomerhalder	khloekardashian	normancook	msleamichele
ijessewilliams	iamdiddy	champagnepapi	aliciakeys
instagranph	popsugar	mindykaling	reesewitherspoon
itsashbenzo	emmaroberts	jaime_king	jessicaalba
jaime_king	jessicaalba	emmaroberts	itsashbenzo

In order to provide the recommendation on whom to follow, we can compare the most similar users. From the preceding example, we can see that the user `aliciakeys` is most similar to `johnlegend`, so we compare both of them to arrive at a recommendation. To provide a recommendation to `aliciakeys`, we check the people whom `johnlegend` follows, but not `aliciakeys`, and provide those users as a recommendation to `aliciakeys`. We can write the recommendations computed to a file so that it can be supplied as input to any other system. Similar to this user-based recommendation, we can also implement item-based filtering. The decision to choose the user-based filtering or the item-based filtering should be taken based on the number of users and items. For example, when the number of users are more than the number of items, then it is better to go ahead with the item-based filtering approach. If the number of items are more than the number of users, we need to implement the user-based filtering.

Improvements to the recommendation system

We can compute the similarity based on the use of multiple methods and finally combine them to form an ensemble algorithm. We can also implement the hybrid methodology, which combines the user-based method as well as the item-based methods.

We will also introduce the concept of classification, that is, dividing the dataset into different groups and build recommendation engines for each of them. Generally, this improves the accuracy, as the recommendations are customized to the groups.

Exercise:

We have seen the implementation of the recommendation engine. Now, try the following exercises:

- Compute the similarity between the users using the Pearson methodology and give 50 percent weightage to both the methods.
- For the preceding dataset, try to implement the item-based recommendation. Instead of identifying the similarity between the users, identify the similarity between the items (in this case, it is the user accounts followed by our celebrity users).

Business case

Some of the business cases that can be implemented using the Instagram data are as follows:

- Provide recommendations to users on places to travel

- Determine visitor trends to various tourist locations

- Find out what people say about various locations

- Determine the performance of various media posts and create a time series trend for them

- Find out the popularity trend of various celebrity users and brands on Instagram

- Compare Instagram popularity scores of brands with that of their competitors

Reference

- Amazon's *Item-to-Item Collaborative Filtering.*

  `http://www.cs.umd.edu/~samir/498/Amazon-Recommendations.pdf`

- More about clustering analysis

  `http://www.statmethods.net/advstats/cluster.html`

- About the package `instaR`

  `https://github.com/pablobarbera/instaR/tree/master/instaR`

- Online courses

  `https://www.coursera.org/course/clusteranalysis`

  `https://class.coursera.org/ml-003/lecture/100`

- Celebrity users and the location hashtags were obtained from here:

  `https://socialblade.com/instagram/top/100/followers`

  `http://www.popsugar.com/celebrity/Celebrities-Using-Instagram-21244293?stream_view=1#photo-23154687`

  `http://top-hashtags.com/hashtag/monument/`

Summary

In this chapter, we covered the procedure involved in creation of an app on the Instagram platform. We covered the sequential steps for authentication and accessing the data from R using the package `instaR`. We also acquired competency to build a dataset of users and location from the Instagram platform.

We discussed the skill of using the collected data to solve critical business problems. Some of the problems that we have solved include identifying the popular users based on multiple metrics, exploring the destinations which people talk about the most, dividing the dataset into different groups by applying a clustering algorithm, building a recommendation system using the collaborative filtering algorithm on who the users might be interested to follow based on the behavior of similar users, and finally a quick brief about the various other business cases that could be solved using the Instagram data.

In the next chapter we will be learning about the implementation of some of the graphical and non-graphical EDA techniques such as histogram, pie chart, box plot, correlations and much more by using a heterogeneous dataset created by way of the GitHub API from R.

5
Let's Build Software with GitHub

GitHub is a Web-based Git repository hosting service and it offers distributed revision control, source code management functionality of Git, and much more. GitHub supports both private and public repositories. There are a vast number of public projects in GitHub to which contributions come from multiple people around the world. GitHub provides an API to access their data; the public data can be accessed by anyone whereas the private data can be accessed only by authorized users.

In this chapter, we will see how to access the public data of GitHub using its API from R, and we will see how to perform **Exploratory Data Analysis (EDA)** and mine significant patterns from the GitHub data extracted by us. As a part of this chapter, we will cover different methods to extract the data from GitHub and various graphical and non-graphical EDA techniques.

The objectives of this chapter are to show how to extract the public data from GitHub and focus on getting a better understanding of various EDA techniques, detecting anomalies, and extracting patterns from the data. We will start from the basics of EDA and discuss a few advanced visualizations that will be useful for getting answers to some interesting questions such as getting to know the most popular language, user comparison with other users, trends on updates made to the public repositories, different programming languages and their affinity towards one another, and much more.

The topics that will be covered in this chapter are as follows:

- Creating an app on GitHub
- GitHub package installation and authentication
- Accessing GitHub data from R

- Building a heterogeneous dataset of the most active users
- Building additional metrics
- Introduction to exploratory data analysis
- EDA — graphical analysis
- EDA — correlation analysis

Creating an app on GitHub

We need to register a new application on GitHub in order to access the public GitHub data from R with authentication. In Facebook, creating an app to access the data is not mandatory and we can generate a temporary token to access most of the data. In GitHub, we can access data without authentication but with a limitation on the number of calls that can be made, whereas authentication provides the access we need.

In order to create a GitHub app, we need to log in as a developer in GitHub. Go to `https://developer.github.com/program/` and log in as a developer:

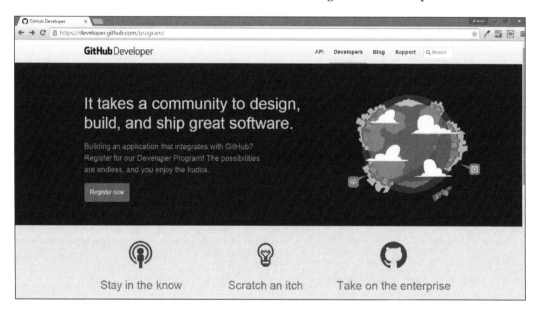

Click on the **Register now** button in the page and you can choose to pay and buy a developer login. The free account user cannot register as a developer. Alternatively, you can use an existing account and login.

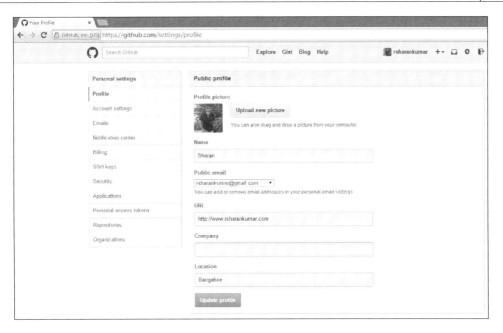

In this case, I logged in using an existing public account. To create an app, we need to click on the **settings** icon in the top-right corner of the page. You should be able to see your **profile page** as shown in the preceding screenshot. To create a new application, we need to click on the **Applications** link that appears on the left-hand side of the panel and then click on the **Developer applications** tab. Now, you will see a **Register new application** button.

Click on **Register new application** and the following page will open. Give a suitable name for the app and fill in other mandatory details. In the **Authorization Callback URL** textbox, please enter the following URL: `http://localhost:1410`. This is the call back URL that GitHub will return to after successful authentication of the app. Finally, confirm the creation of the app. This new app can be used to access all the public data, including the public repositories of other users.

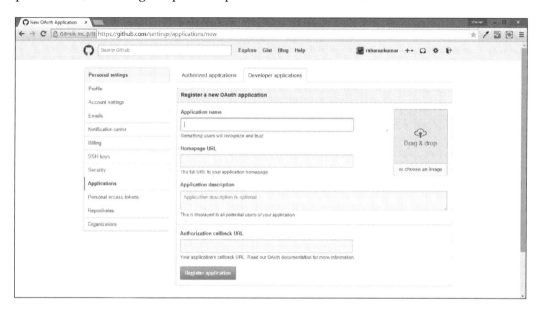

Once you have registered your app, the **Client ID** and **Client Secret** values will be generated. These values will be unique to your app. Please be careful with these keys and don't share them with others or post them in the public forum. Now we are ready. From R, use the ID and key to get access to the public data. If necessary you can also generate a new secret key by clicking on the **Reset client secret** button or you can also choose to revoke access to the app by clicking on the **Revoke all user tokens**.

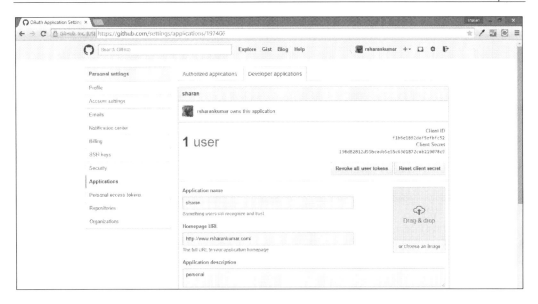

GitHub package installation and authentication

We will use GitHub API Version 3 for accessing the data. All the API access that happens is over HTTPS and it is accessed from the domain `api.github.com` or `yourdomain.com/api/v3` for the enterprise accounts. All the data received will be in the JSON format.

Now that you know how to create a GitHub app, we will see how to proceed further towards accessing the data from R. In order to connect to the GitHub app, we need to install the `rgithub` package and other dependent packages like `devtools`. The `devtools` package is required so that we can install the latest `rgithub` package directly from the source.

```
require(devtools)
install_github("cscheid/rgithub")
library(github)
```

After the installation and loading the required packages in R, we can use the client ID and the client secret that were generated to authenticate the access. In the following example, we are first passing the client ID and the client secret to a variable and then using the function `interactive.login` along with the `client.id` and `client.secret` parameters to authenticate the access.

```
# Authentication
client.id <- "paste your App's ID here"
client.secret<- "paste your secret key here"
ctx = interactive.login(client.id, client.secret)
```

On executing the preceding line, we might be prompted with the following question about caching the credentials. We have an option to cache the credentials into a local file so that it can be used to login for later R sessions. Otherwise, we need to authenticate each R session. I would prefer not to save the credentials to a file hence I would enter my preference as 2 or No. Then, you will be redirected to the GitHub website after authenticating the process.

```
> ctx = interactive.login(client.id, client.secret)
Use a local file to cache OAuth access credentials between R sessions?
1: Yes
2: No

Selection:
```

On successful completion of all the steps, we will get the following message:

```
Waiting for authentication in browser...
Press Esc/Ctrl + C to abort
Authentication complete.
```

After completing the authentication, we are ready to go ahead and access the public data available in GitHub. This would include the public repositories, public user profiles, followers, and other details related to repositories, contributions, commits, and users. In order to know more about the API, kindly visit `https://developer.github.com/v3/`.

Exercise:
Create an app in GitHub and authenticate from R.

Accessing GitHub data from R

Accessing the GitHub data from R is simple. It can be accessed using the package `rgithub` developed by Carlos Scheidegger, which provides the binding for the GitHub web services API. We can also use the API URL directly in the function `fromJSON`, which will extract the JSON data in data frame format.

Previously, we saw how to authenticate using the package `rgithub`; now let's use some of the functions available in the package to pull data from GitHub.

First, let's pull our GitHub account data using the function `get.myself` and pass the variable `ctx` as a parameter, which is a GitHub context object holding the authentication results. This function will provide basic details about our account such as date created, last updated, location, e-mail, number of public repositories contributed, following and followers, and also about the number of API calls we have made in the current session. Let's execute the function `get.myself` and check the output.

```
get.myself(ctx)
```

We get the following output:

```
$ok
[1] TRUE

$content
$content$login
[1] "rsharankumar"

$content$id
[1] 3078066

$content$avatar_url
[1] "https://avatars.githubusercontent.com/u/3078066?v=3"

$content$gravatar_id
[1] ""

$content$url
[1] "https://api.github.com/users/rsharankumar"

$content$html_url
[1] "https://github.com/rsharankumar"

$content$followers_url
[1] "https://api.github.com/users/rsharankumar/followers"
```

Here are a few more functions that can be used to pull additional information:

- `get.my.repositories(ctx)`
- `get.my.following(ctx)`
- `get.public.events(ctx)`

The function `get.my.repositories` will get the details of the repositories created by us and the function `get.my.following` will provide details about the people following us on GitHub. The result of all calls to the API is requested as HTTP and the response is automatically parsed into JSON, the message format used throughout the API. All the functions in the package will start with a verb, followed by the appropriate object. We will also extract the random public repositories of others users. This can be achieved using the function `get.all.repositories`. By default, the function would get the details of random 100 public repositories:

```
get.all.repositories(ctx = get.github.context())
```

Also, visit `https://github.com/cscheid/rgithub` to learn more about the other functions implemented in the package.

Exercise

- Extract the public repositories of a few active users and identify their languages capability.
- Identify if they have common followers.
- Filter the repositories that are currently having open issues.

Building a heterogeneous dataset using the most active users

Let's build a heterogeneous dataset based on the public repositories created by the most active users of GitHub. As we know how to extract data using the package `rgithub`, we will explore the other method too, for example, directly using the API's URL. In this method, we need to pass the API URL to the function `fromJSON`, which has a dependency on the package `jsonlite`. The API URL will also work from the browser and will be checked for accuracy of the data. Those URLs will return data in JSON format.

The most active users of GitHub will be obtained through the following URL, or you can use the CSV file named `TopUsers.csv`, which also holds the data of users who were active as of July 2015. We will make use of the username to pull the additional data about the users.

Use the function `read.csv` to read the active users file from `https://gist.github.com/paulmillr/2657075/` and read the username column as characters using the function `as.character`. Now, the usernames of the active users are present in the object named `uname`:

```
topuser<- read.csv("TopUsers.csv")
uname<- as.character(topuser$Username)
```

In the following code, we are looping through the usernames to extract all the data about the public repositories published by those users. The `for` loop might fail for certain users and during those times the loop would break. In such cases, we can get the counter number when it failed and rerun the loop, starting with the value `Failed Counter + 1`. The code is as follows:

```
library(jsonlite)
library(stringr)
compdata <- ""
for (i in 1:nrow(topuser))
{
data2<- fromJSON(paste0("https://api.github.com/users/",
str_trim(uname[i], side = "both"),
"/repos?client_id=paste_your_client_id_here&client_secret=
paste_your_key_here"))
   data2 <- data2[,-(4)]
compdata<- rbind(compdata, data2)
print(i)
}
```

The URL for pulling the repository would follow the following format, where `rsharankumar` is a username. All the usernames are unique.

By passing `https://api.github.com/users/rsharankumar/repos` we will be able to access the GitHub data of just 60 users as only 60 requests are permitted in an hour for unauthenticated access. By passing the `client_id` and `client_secret` values to the preceding URL we will be able to make 5000 requests in an hour. This can be achieved by making a few modifications to the URL.

In `https://api.github.com/users/hadley/repos?client_id=paste_id_here&client_secret=paste_key_here`, we have to pass the username dynamically, which can be achieved using the function `paste0`. We use `paste0` to avoid the whitespace between the strings and then use the `rbind` function to consolidate all the user's data. In general, `for` loops are time-consuming, hence we will print `i` to check the progress of the loop. Finally, we can write an aggregation function to write the aggregated data into a file so that it can be reused. Let this aggregated file be the master file with all the details and let's perform the data operations on top of this file:

```
write.csv(compdata, file ="ActiveUsers.csv")
```

Data processing

Though we have extracted the active user's data, it is not ready for usage. We need to perform a few data processing operations to make it ready to use for the analysis. Use the following code to read the master copy of the data which was saved by us:

```
activeusers<- read.csv("ActiveUsers.csv")
```

We need to change the date format so that it will be supported by R. This can be accomplished using the following function. It is better to use a function in this case because there are multiple date columns that need to be changed; hence, this function will reduce code redundancy. Since the time zone of the data is in *GMT*, we set the parameter `tz` to GMT. In your case, if the time zone corresponds to your present time zone, it should be set as empty double quotes:

```
# Change date to format supported by R
format.git.date<- function(datestring) {
date<- as.POSIXct(datestring, format = "%Y-%m-%dT%H:%M:%SZ",
tz = "GMT")
}
```

The preceding function is required to convert the date format of three columns. Execute the following code to make the changes to the date format of the columns `created_at`, `updated_at` and `pushed_at`, which holds the information of the date on which the repository was created, last updated, as well as last pushed:

```
# Updating the column with new date format
activeusers$created_at<- format.git.date(activeusers$created_at)
activeusers$updated_at<- format.git.date(activeusers$updated_at)
activeusers$pushed_at<- format.git.date(activeusers$pushed_at)
```

The data frame `activeusers` holds additional URL data which is not required for the analysis that will be performed as a part of this chapter. Hence, we will select only the required columns through the column selection method. First, we use the function `colnames` to learn all the column names as well as their position, and then we use the respective column number to subset the required data:

```
# Subsetting required data
# To check which columns to select
colnames(activeusers)
# Selecting the required data
```

```
ausersubset <-
activeusers[,c("id","name","full_name","private","description",
"fork","created_at","updated_at","pushed_at","homepage","size",
"stargazers_count","watchers_count","language","has_issues",
"has_downloads","has_wiki","has_pages","forks_count",
"open_issues_count","forks","open_issues","watchers")]
```

We need to format the columns that hold values TRUE and FALSE to 1 and 0, respectively, so that the analysis will be simpler. This can be achieved simply by using the function as.integer. Execute the following code to format all the required columns:

```
# Replace True and False with 1 and 0
ausersubset$private<- as.integer(ausersubset$private)
ausersubset$fork<- as.integer(ausersubset$fork)
ausersubset$has_issues<- as.integer(ausersubset$has_issues)
ausersubset$has_downloads<- as.integer(ausersubset$has_downloads)
ausersubset$has_wiki<- as.integer(ausersubset$has_wiki)
ausersubset$has_pages<- as.integer(ausersubset$has_pages)
```

The column full_name holds the name of the user/account along with the repository name, separated by the symbol /. We use the strsplit function to extract the username alone. In the following code, we replace the username with the same column. Finally, we use the head function to check if the output is in line with the expectation:

```
# Getting the username
ausersubset$full_name<-
sapply(strsplit(as.character(ausersubset$full_name),
split='/', fixed=TRUE), function(x) (x[1]))
head(ausersubset$full_name)
```

Building additional metrics

We completed the data formatting part, and processed the data so that it can be used for our analysis. Before going to the analysis bit, let's see how to construct a few metrics, which will become a derived column in our dataset. Let's write code to create the following metrics:

1. Identify if there is a web page associated with the repository.
2. Count the number of characters in the description.
3. Identify how long it had been since the repository was created, updated, and pushed.

To identify if there is a website associated with the repository, we need to look at the column homepage. We will use the function grepl to identify the presence of a dot in the column homepage, which we would consider a proxy for the presence of a website entry, as this column either holds the website details or an empty string/number.

```
# Flag for presence of website/webpage
ausersubset$has_web<- as.numeric(grepl(".", ausersubset$homepage))
```

The preceding code will create a new column named has_web and will hold a value 1, indicating the presence of a website or web page for the repository, or 0, which indicates no entries for a website or web page.

To count the number of characters in the description, we need to convert the description into characters using the function as.character, and then the number of characters can be counted using the function nchar. The number of characters will be stored in the new column desclen:

```
# Length of the description
ausersubset$desclen<- nchar(as.character(ausersubset$description))
```

We need to identify how long it has been since the repository was created, updated, and pushed. First, we use the function Sys.Date() to get the current date and then use the function difftime to get the day difference. Execute the following code to get the new metrics on the day difference:

```
# Day difference from current date for created, updated and pushed
ausersubset$dayscreated<-
as.integer(difftime(Sys.Date(),ausersubset$created_at ,
units = c("days")))
ausersubset$daysupdated<-
as.integer(difftime(Sys.Date(),ausersubset$updated_at ,
units = c("days")))
ausersubset$dayspushed<-
as.integer(difftime(Sys.Date(),ausersubset$pushed_at ,
units = c("days")))
```

After creating all the required metrics, use the function head to check the format of the data:

```
head(ausersubset)
```

We get the following output:

```
> head(ausersubset)
        id          name full_name private
1 20219396        AdminLTE  Ocramius       0
2 10198601     annotations  Ocramius       0
3 20619143          Ardent  Ocramius       0
4 11644698           Artax  Ocramius       0
5 12464701 asm89.github.com Ocramius       0
6  5399871    AssetManager  Ocramius       0
                                                          description
1 AdminLTE - Free Premium Admin control Panel Theme That Is Based On Bootstrap 3.x
2                                               Annotations Docblock Parser
3                                               A Collections library for PHP.
4                                 An object-oriented HTTP/1.1 Client for PHP 5.4+
5
6                                 An asset manager module for zend framework 2
  fork          created_at          updated_at           pushed_at
1    1 2014-05-27 12:35:28 2015-02-07 06:03:20 2014-05-05 13:14:09
2    1 2013-05-21 15:10:28 2014-04-21 20:01:42 2014-12-20 20:55:11
3    1 2014-06-08 15:09:17 2014-06-08 23:15:01 2014-06-08 15:09:29
4    1 2013-07-24 20:37:20 2014-09-24 16:46:55 2013-08-12 12:16:55
5    1 2013-05-29 15:59:11 2013-11-25 22:21:43 2013-11-25 22:05:43
6    1 2012-08-13 14:18:58 2014-03-26 07:30:23 2014-03-25 19:02:46
                         homepage  size stargazers_count watchers_count
1       http://www.almsaeedstudio.com  6280                3              3
2                            <NA> 13603                0              0
3                                  778                0              0
4 http://rdlowrey.github.com/Artax/  2434                0              0
5                            <NA>  2106                0              0
6                            <NA>   471                1              1
   language has_issues has_downloads has_wiki has_pages forks_count
1 JavaScript          0             1        1         0           4
2        PHP          0             1        0         0           0
3        PHP          0             1        0         0           0
4        PHP          0             1        0         0           1
5        CSS          0             1        1         0           0
6        PHP          0             1        1         0           0
  open_issues_count forks open_issues watchers has_web desclen dayscreated
1                 0     4           0        3       1      80         388
```

Note that the preceding screenshot is just a part of the output.

Exercise:

- In addition to the preceding dataset, each user will also have information such as the number of followers as well as the number of accounts the user is following.
- For all the preceding repositories, identify the subscribers.
- Identify how many times the repositories were committed and how many unique users were involved in the commits with a comparison to the number of contributors.

Exploratory data analysis

EDA techniques are used for discovering patterns in the data, summarization, as well as for visualization of the data. It is an essential step in the data analysis process, which helps to formulate various hypotheses about the data.

The EDA techniques shall be broadly classified into three types: *univariate*, *bivariate*, and *multivariate* analysis. Let's implement a few of the EDA techniques on our dataset.

First, let's see what kind of data we are analyzing. Using the function `sapply`, we determine the various columns present in the dataset and the datatype of those columns:

```
sapply(ausersubset, class)
```

We get the following output:

```
$fork
[1] "integer"

$created_at
[1] "POSIXct" "POSIXt"

$updated_at
[1] "POSIXct" "POSIXt"

$pushed_at
[1] "POSIXct" "POSIXt"

$homepage
[1] "factor"

$size
[1] "integer"
```

 Note that the preceding screenshot is just a part of the output.

In order to get a basic understanding of the whole dataset, such as the distribution of the values of the columns, we can use the `summary` function to get the highlights of the dataset. For example, we will get the minimum, mean, median, maximum, and quartile values for each column:

```
summary(ausersubset)
```

We get the following output:

```
  pushed_at                                      homepage           size
Min.   :2008-03-26 19:11:40                              :2307   Min.   :       0
1st Qu.:2012-12-26 13:19:09   https://gjcampbell.co.uk/:  19   1st Qu.:     132
Median :2014-04-10 06:33:50   http://angularjs.org      :  10   Median :     287
Mean   :2013-10-31 19:39:02   http://bower.io           :  10   Mean   :   10269
3rd Qu.:2015-02-05 10:09:00   http://webtorrent.io      :  10   3rd Qu.:    1323
Max.   :2015-06-16 19:34:32   (Other)                   :2076   Max.   :8134718
NA's   :14                    NA's                      :2712
 stargazers_count    watchers_count          language          has_issues
Min.   :    0.00   Min.   :    0.00   JavaScript:2183   Min.   :0.000
1st Qu.:    0.00   1st Qu.:    0.00   Ruby      : 658   1st Qu.:0.000
Median :    2.00   Median :    2.00   Python    : 508   Median :1.000
Mean   :   82.67   Mean   :   82.67   PHP       : 443   Mean   :0.585
3rd Qu.:   10.00   3rd Qu.:   10.00   CSS       : 265   3rd Qu.:1.000
Max.   :40586.00   Max.   :40586.00   (Other)   :2240   Max.   :1.000
                                      NA's      : 847
 has_downloads      has_wiki          has_pages        forks_count
Min.   :0.0000   Min.   :0.0000   Min.   :0.000   Min.   :   0.00
1st Qu.:1.0000   1st Qu.:1.0000   1st Qu.:0.000   1st Qu.:   0.00
Median :1.0000   Median :1.0000   Median :0.000   Median :   0.00
Mean   :0.9763   Mean   :0.8515   Mean   :0.148   Mean   :  17.66
3rd Qu.:1.0000   3rd Qu.:1.0000   3rd Qu.:0.000   3rd Qu.:   2.00
Max.   :1.0000   Max.   :1.0000   Max.   :1.000   Max.   :9242.00
```

 Note that the preceding screenshot is just a part of the output.

Let's now find the standard deviation for all the numeric columns in the dataset using the function `apply`. All the non-numeric columns in the dataset would come as NA. Other techniques are also used for EDA. We will use a few of those graphical, as well as non-graphical, techniques on this GitHub data to get a better understanding:

```
apply(ausersubset, 2, sd)
```

We get the following output:

pushed_at	homepage	size	stargazers_count
NA	NA	1.321590e+05	7.694698e+02
watchers_count	language	has_issues	has_downloads
7.694698e+02	NA	4.927623e-01	1.519863e-01
has_wiki	has_pages	forks_count	open_issues_count
3.556359e-01	3.550815e-01	2.163168e+02	1.723065e+01
forks	open_issues	watchers	has_web
2.163168e+02	1.723065e+01	7.694698e+02	4.571693e-01

Note that the preceding screenshot is just a part of the output.

Exercise

- Identify the skewness and kurtosis for the numeric columns from the preceding dataset.
- Use the functions `skewness` and `kurtosis` of the package `moments`.
- Identify all of the preceding measures after removing the outliers in the data and see how much it differs.

EDA – graphical analysis

"A picture is worth a thousand words."

Graphical analysis is quite popular, as it helps people grasp the content faster. The existence of so many dashboard tools in the market is also proof of this. With the recent innovation in the field of visualization, it is certainly one of the best mediums of communication.

In this section, let's explore a few graphical EDA. The graphical EDA techniques will help us get a more penetrative understanding of the data and also help in presenting complicated statistical analysis in a more understandable format. We will use some of the visualization packages in R that will help in making the output look better.

Which language is most popular among the active GitHub users?

We have the data at the repository level. Each repository is a project that could have been implemented in any language. Let's present the language data in a graphical format and understand the popularity. First, we will use the function `table` to see how many languages are used and how many times they are being used:

```
table(ausersubset$language)
```

We get the following output:

ActionScript	Agda	ApacheConf
13	2	3
Apex	Arduino	ASP
1	5	1
Assembly	ATS	AutoHotkey
3	1	1
Batchfile	C	C#
1	207	84
C++	Clojure	CMake
118	79	1
CoffeeScript	Common Lisp	Coq
122	13	2
Crystal	CSS	Dart
1	265	15
DIGITAL Command Language	Elixir	Elm
1	10	19
Emacs Lisp	Erlang	Gnuplot
90	20	1
Go	Gosu	Groff
205	1	1
Groovy	Haskell	Haxe
8	111	1
HaXe	HTML	Ioke
3	104	1
Java	JavaScript	Julia
255	2183	2

 Note that preceding screenshot is just a part of the output.

Though the tabular representation of the data provides us with the required information, it becomes difficult to understand the relative popularity of the languages. Hence, a graphical view of the same data is required. We will use the histogram function, using the packages ggplot2 to see the distribution of various languages:

```
q <- qplot(ausersubset$language,
geom="histogram",
binwidth = 1,
main = "Histogram for Language",
xlab = "Language",
fill=I("blue"),
col=I("red"))
```

The preceding code will plot the histogram based on the column `language`. However, since there are many different languages, the labels would overlap each other. It would be difficult to read the plot with the overlapping labels, so we use the parameter `theme` and set the text angle to 90 degrees to make the labels appear vertical and avoid overlapping. The following plot can be saved using the function `ggsave`:

```
q + theme(axis.text.x = element_text(angle = 90, hjust = 1))
ggsave(file="C:/Users/Sharan/Desktop/SMM/Chapter
5/Pics/language.png", dpi=500)
```

We get the following output:

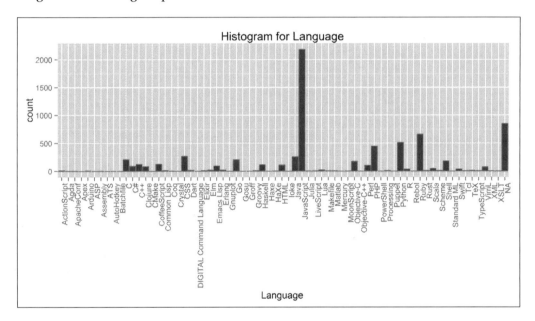

From the preceding graph, we understand that the spread of the languages is wide but there are a few languages that are very popular. We find that the most popular language among the active users is JavaScript, and more than 2000 repositories are developed using JavaScript. Also, it now becomes easy for us to learn the relative popularity. Through visualization, we can make out that out of the 68 different languages only 23 have been used in at least 20 plus repositories.

Because of the presence of many languages in the dataset as well as the skewness in the dataset, it becomes difficult to notice the difference between the counts for the other top languages. Hence, we filter the most popular languages and plot a bar chart only for those languages. The code is as follows:

```
# Bar chart for the top languages
a <- table(ausersubset$language)
```

```
a <- as.data.frame(a)
a <- a[with(a, order(-Freq)), ]
toplang<- a[2:21,]
colnames(toplang) <- c("Language","Count")
```

The preceding code first converts the data in the tabular format to a data frame, then we use the function `order` to sort the data in descending order, and then we filter the top 21 languages, except the topmost language, that is, JavaScript, to avoid skewness in the result. After filtering the data we use the following code to draw a bar chart of the top languages. Thus, we have a clearer view on the use of the other top languages in the repositories. The code is as follows:

```
q <- qplot(x=Language, y=Count,
data=toplang, geom="bar", stat="identity",
position="dodge")
q + theme(axis.text.x = element_text(angle = 90, hjust = 1))
```

We get the following output:

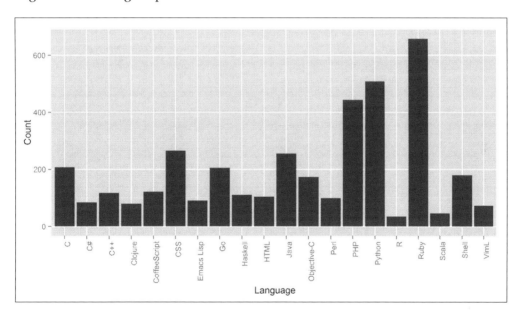

What is the distribution of watchers, forks, and issues in GitHub?

In the introduction to the EDA section, we already saw the distribution of all the columns in the dataset. Now, we will see how it would be to view it in a graphical representation. We will use the box plot to explore the distribution of the dataset.

First, let's perform a *univariate* analysis and have a look at the variables one at a time. We will analyze the variables Watchers_Count, Forks_Count, Open_Issues and Stargazers. We will draw the box plot using the following function:

```
boxplot(ausersubset$watchers_count, outline = FALSE)
boxplot(ausersubset$forks_count, outline = FALSE)
boxplot(ausersubset$open_issues, outline = FALSE)
boxplot(ausersubset$stargazers_count, outline = FALSE)
```

The preceding code will plot the variables one by one. We can also have them together in a single chart across the same scale to gain a better comparison using the following code. Due to the presence of a large number of outliers, we will disable it from appearing to the plots by setting the parameter outline to FALSE:

```
forbplot<- ausersubset[c("watchers_count", "forks_count",
"open_issues", "stargazers_count")]
boxplot(forbplot, outline = FALSE)
```

We get the following output:

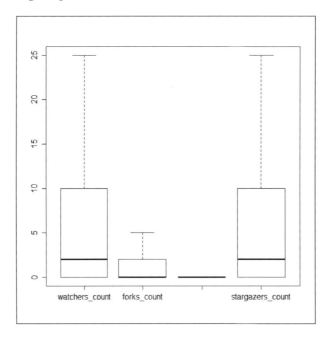

From the preceding plot, we understand that the distribution of the variables watchers_count and startgazers_count is very similar. Also, the distribution of the variable open_issues is almost equal to zero. This suggests that the repositories are healthy.

Now, we will perform a *bivariate* analysis using the boxplot. We will consider the variable `watchers_count` and see how it trends across the variable `open_issues_count`. We use the following code for plotting, and we have set the parameter `notch` to `TRUE` to see if the plot is overlapping or not:

```
library(reshape2)
colnames(ausersubset)
dat.m<- melt(ausersubset, id.vars='open_issues_count',
measure.vars=c('watchers_count'))
library(ggplot2)
p <- ggplot(dat.m) +
geom_boxplot(aes(x=open_issues_count, y=value, color=variable),
outlier.shape = NA, notch = TRUE, notchwidth= 0.5) +
scale_y_continuous(limits = quantile(ausersubset$stargazers_count,
c(0, 0.6)))
ggsave(file="C:/Users/Sharan/Desktop/SMM/Chapter 5/Pics/boxplot-bi.
png", dpi=500)
```

We get the following output:

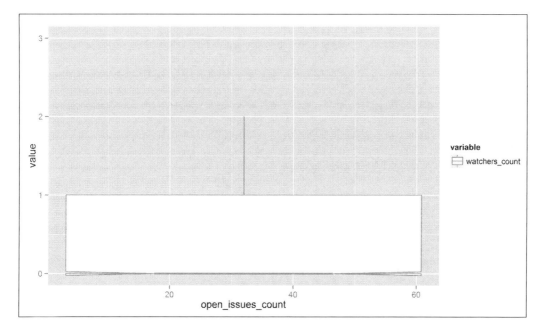

The overlapping in the preceding box plot clearly proves to us that the median of the variable `watchers_count` doesn't differ much across the range of the variable `open_issues_count`.

How many repositories had issues?

A pie chart is a data presentation technique where the data is represented in the form of circle, where the circle will be in turn divided into multiple segments. Each segment represents a certain proportion or percentage of the total. Though a pie chart is a popular graphical representation among sales teams as well as print and digital media, it has some limitations:

- It can represent only one continuous variable.
- It occupies too much space.
- It is difficult to compare and interpret multiple pie charts

Let's use the pie chart to understand how many of the repositories had issues. In the following code, we have used the ggplot function to draw the pie chart:

```
# Pie chart: Issues in the repositary
pie<- ggplot(ausersubset, aes(x = factor(1), fill =
factor(ausersubset$has_issues))) + geom_bar(width = 1)
pie + coord_polar(theta = "y") =
ggsave(file="C:/Users/Sharan/Desktop/SMM/Chapter 5/
Pics/pie-chart.png", dpi=500)
```

We get the following output:

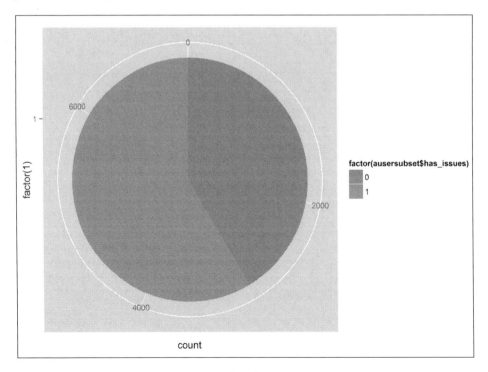

In the preceding pie chart, `1` represents the repositories which had issues, and `0` represents those that did not have any issues. From the preceding chart, it is clear that the majority of the repositories had issues at some point in time.

What is the trend on updating repositories?

Trend analysis is a method of analysis that helps us in understanding the patterns in a parameter across time. We can get a clear view on the trend of the dataset. Let's perform trend analysis through a line chart.

We will consider only the columns `updated_at` and `id` for this analysis. After updating the new data frame with the following values, we will convert the date time into date format using the function `as.POSIXct` and we will consolidate the data to a daily level using the function `table`:

```
library(data.table)
trenddata<- ausersubset[c("updated_at", "id")]
trenddata$updated_at<-
as.POSIXct(strptime(trenddata$updated_at, "%Y-%m-%d"))
tdata<- table(trenddata$updated_at)
```

The data needs to be converted to the data frame format and then we can rename the columns for ease of readability. For this analysis, let's consider the data around a recent time period; let's consider only the last 75 days, data:

```
tdata<- as.data.frame(tdata)
colnames(tdata) <- c("Date","Repositories")
tdata$Date <- as.Date(tdata$Date)
tdata1 <- tail(tdata, 75)
```

Finally, we will plot the trend chart using the function `ggplot` and with the help of additional parameters such as `geom_line` and `geom_point`, we can make the chart better looking as well as more communicative:

```
q <- ggplot(data=tdata1, aes(x=Date, y=Repositories, group=1)) +
geom_line() +
geom_point()
q + theme(axis.text.x = element_text(angle = 90, hjust = 1))
ggsave(file="C:/Users/Sharan/Desktop/SMM/Chapter 5/Pics/
line-chart.png", dpi=500)
```

We get the following output:

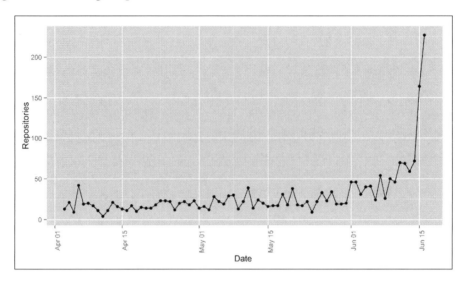

From the preceding line chart, we see that a vast number of repositories were updated in recent days and more than 200 repositories were updated on the last day. Also, very few repositories have been without any updates for a long time.

Compare users through heat map

Heat map is a popular visualization tool. It is one of the best tools for *multivariate* and *timeseries* analysis and helps us in comparing the multiple variables visually. We will learn to use the heat map to study the GitHub users. First, we will aggregate some information at the user level and then compare it across multiple users. We will consider the following variables to perform this analysis at the user level and perform aggregation based on the variable at the user level (full_name).

Variable	Aggregation	Details
full_name	N.A.	User's name
id	Count	Number of repositories
Size	Average	Average size of repositories
Watchers_count	Sum	Total Watchers to user's repositories
forks_count	Sum	Total Forks to his repositories
open_issues_count	Sum	Total Issues in his repositories
desclen	Average	Average length of title description
dayscreated	Average	Average age of user's repositories

Variable	Aggregation	Details
daysupdated	Average	Average time since last updated
dayspushed	Average	Average time since last push

The preceding data selection is performed using the following code by selecting the desired columns from the master dataset and moving it to the new dataset named newdata. The aggregations are then performed using the SQL query. In order to use the SQL query, we need to load the package sqldf using the library function and then write the following query to the function sqldf:

```
colnames(ausersubset)
library(sqldf)
newdata<- ausersubset[c("id","full_name","size","watchers_count",
"forks_count", "open_issues_count", "desclen", "dayscreated",
"daysupdated", "dayspushed")]
sd<- sqldf("select full_name, count(id), avg(size),
sum(watchers_count), count(forks_count), count(open_issues_count),
avg(desclen), avg(dayscreated), avg(daysupdated), avg(dayspushed)
from newdata group by full_name")
```

Now, we have the data in the required format, we can give the desired name to the metrics created in the new data frame using the colnames function. For plotting the heat map, we will consider only a subset of the data, since it would be impossible to visualize and interpret the heat map for all the users at the same time. We will sort the users based on the number of repositories in descending order and select the top 40 users for the visualization:

```
colnames(sd) <- c("Name", "Repositories", "AverageSize",
"Watchers", "Forks", "Issues", "Avg_desc_length",
"Avg_days_since_created", "Avg_days_since_updated",
"Avg_days_since_pushed")
row.names(sd) <- sd$Name
sd<- sd[order(-sd$Repositories),]
sd<- sd[1:40,]
```

We will select the numeric columns in the dataset and then convert the dataset into a matrix so that we can plot using the function heatmap. We will then copy the image to the system using the dev.copy function. After copying the image, it is always advisable to switch it off using the function dev.off. The code is as follows:

```
names(sd)
sd<- sd[,2:10]
sdmat<- as.matrix(sd)
sd_heatmap<- heatmap(sdmat, Rowv=NA, Colv=NA, col =
cm.colors(256), scale="column", margins=c(5,8))
```

```
dev.copy(png,filename="C:/Users/Sharan/Desktop/SMM/Chapter
5/Pics/heatmap-users.png", width=600, height=875);
dev.off ();
```

Using the heat map, we get a quick understanding about the users. The shade towards red indicates a higher value and towards green indicates a lower value, while white indicates the value lies in the median. With a glance at the heat map, we can easily answer the following questions about the users:

- Which user has got the highest number of repositories?

- Which user has got a comparatively higher number of watchers?

- How many of those users have been relatively inactive?

- Which users have the most, as well as the least, issues open in their repositories?

Also, this view will give us an idea about the correlation between different parameters about the users. For example, from the following output, we can see the average days since creation, as well as the average days since it has been pushed, have a higher correlation between them, as they share a similar color pattern. Similarly, there seems to be a strong relationship between the Issues, Watcher, and Forks variables.

We get the following output:

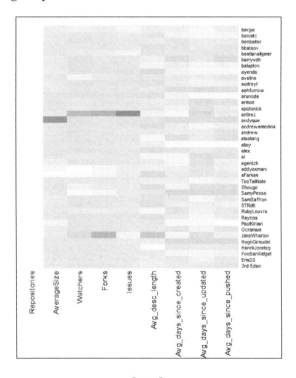

Exercise
- Plot a multiseries line chart using the preceding GitHub dataset.
- Implement a heat map on the date column to prove that heat map can be a good visualization tool for time series datasets.
- Plot a pie chart with percentages instead of values.
- Write the box plot code to include the outlier data and see how the visualization appears.

EDA – correlation analysis

Correlation analysis measures the statistical relationship between two different variables. The result will show how the change in one parameter would impact the other parameter. Correlation analysis is a very important concept, popular in the field of predictive analytics. Also, it is mandatory to complete the correlations analysis before building the model and before arriving at a conclusion about variable relationships. Though correlation analysis helps us in understanding the association between two variables in a dataset, it can't explain, or measure, the cause.

So far, we haven't explored the relationship between different parameters. In this section, we will focus on the *bivariate* and *multivariate* analysis of the GitHub dataset.

We will use the dataset that was created for plotting the heat map to perform the correlation analysis. The following code will get us the required dataset:

```
cordata<- ausersubset[c("id","full_name","size","watchers_count",
"forks_count", "open_issues_count", "desclen", "dayscreated",
"daysupdated", "dayspushed")]
cdata<- sqldf("select full_name, count(id), avg(size),
sum(watchers_count), sum(forks_count), sum(open_issues_count),
avg(desclen), avg(dayscreated), avg(daysupdated),
avg(dayspushed) from cordata group by full_name")
colnames(cdata) <- c("Name", "Repositories", "AverageSize",
"Watchers", "Forks", "Issues", "Avg_desc_length",
"Avg_days_since_created", "Avg_days_since_updated",
"Avg_days_since_pushed")
```

First let's check the relationship between the parameters Watchers and Forks. We can identify the relationship between these parameters using the function cor:

```
cor(cdata$Forks, cdata$Watchers)
```

We get the following output:

```
[1] 0.8934664
```

Correlation values will range from -1 to +1, where the positive value indicates a positive relationship between the parameters and the negative value indicates a negative relationship. The positive relationship means that the increase in value of one variable would increase the value of the other variable, whereas in the negative relationship, the increase in one variable would decrease the value in the other variable. In the preceding example, the correlation value of 0.8934 means that the parameters are highly correlated to each other.

How Watchers is related to Forks

The correlation can also be represented in a graphical format using the scatter plot. We will plot the scatter plot using ggplot. The following code will generate the scatter plot where the two variables passed as inputs will be considered as two axes and the values will be plotted.

```
ggplot(cdata, aes(x=Forks, y=Watchers)) +
geom_point(shape=1) +
geom_smooth(method=lm)
ggsave(file="C:/Users/Sharan/Desktop/SMM/Chapter 5/Pics/
scatter-plot.png", dpi=500)
```

We get the following output:

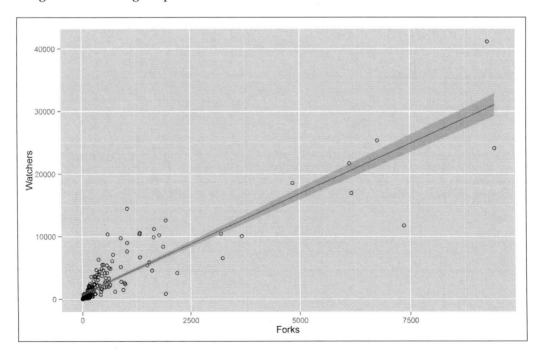

We plotted the relationship between the number of watchers and number of forks for the GitHub users. We saw that these two parameters have a very positive relationship between them though there is a concentration of the values towards the lower range. Also, using the function `geom_smooth` and setting the parameter `method = lm`, we get the regression line with a default confidence region of 95 percent. The regression line tells us that the two parameters have a linear relationship. Let's perform the correlation analysis on a few more parameters and understand the data better.

Correlation with regression line

We have already seen in the heat map that the parameters `Avg_days_since_created` and `Avg_days_since_pushed` seem to have a very good positive relationship. We can test out the same using the correlation function as well as the scatter plot:

```
cor(cdata$Avg_days_since_created, cdata$Avg_days_since_pushed)
```

We get the following output:

```
[1] 0.7899095
```

For generating the scatter plot, use the following code:

```
ggplot(cdata, aes(x=Avg_days_since_created,
y=Avg_days_since_pushed)) +
geom_point(shape=1) +
geom_smooth(method=lm)
ggsave(file="C:/Users/Sharan/Desktop/SMM/Chapter 5/Pics/
scatter-plot2.png", dpi=500)
```

We get the following output:

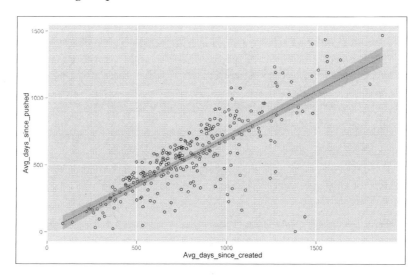

Even in correlation analysis, there is a strong positive relationship between the parameters `Avg_days_since_created` and `Avg_days_since_pushed`. In this case, the values are also widely distributed.

Correlation with local regression curve

We have successfully embedded the linear regression line over the scatter plots but let's try to replace it with the *Loess smoothed fit curve*. This will give us a detailed view and show us how the relationship is at different ranges of values. Let's repeat the preceding plot using this method. In order to bring in the smoothed curve, we use the function `geom_smooth`, the default smoothed curve will be plotted based on the method `loess`. We can change it using the parameter `method`. The code is as follows:

```
ggplot(cdata, aes(x=Avg_days_since_created,
y=Avg_days_since_pushed)) +
geom_point(shape=1) +      # Use hollow circles
geom_smooth()
ggsave(file="C:/Users/Sharan/Desktop/SMM/Chapter 5/Pics/
scatter-plot3.png", dpi=500)
```

We get the following output:

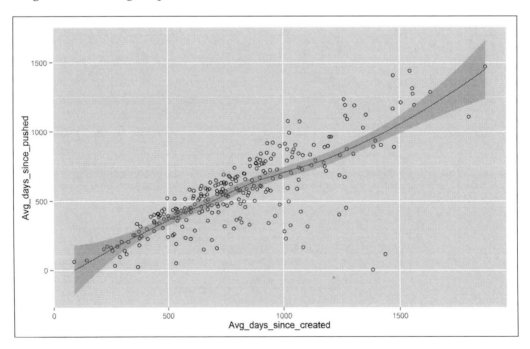

From the preceding plot, we can understand that the relationship is consistent across most of the range of values but towards the higher range it is slightly steeper.

Correlation on segmented data

Now, let's go to the previous scatter plot add a third variable. We will create an `issues` flag, where the users who had less than 10 issues in all the repositories considered together will be flagged as `0`, whereas the other users will be flagged as `1`. This can be implemented through the following code:

```
cordata<- ausersubset[c("id","full_name","size","watchers_count",
"forks_count", "open_issues_count", "desclen", "dayscreated",
"daysupdated", "dayspushed", "has_issues")]
cdata<- sqldf("select full_name, count(id), avg(size),
sum(watchers_count), sum(forks_count), sum(open_issues_count),
avg(desclen), avg(dayscreated), avg(daysupdated), avg(dayspushed),
sum(has_issues) from cordata group by full_name")
colnames(cdata) <- c("Name", "Repositories", "AverageSize",
"Watchers", "Forks", "Issues", "Avg_desc_length",
"Avg_days_since_created", "Avg_days_since_updated",
"Avg_days_since_pushed", "IssuesF")
cdata$IssuesF<- as.factor(cdata$IssuesF)
cdata$IssuesF[cdata$Issues< 10]  = 0
cdata$IssuesF[cdata$Issues>= 10]  = 1
cdata$IssuesF<- as.factor(cdata$IssuesF)
```

After getting the desired data, we will convert the `flag` column to a factor using the function `as.factor`. Now, we will use the plotting function as before, but we will add one more parameter, `color`, to differentiate the different categories. Hence, the first line of the code would be something like this:

```
ggplot(cdata, aes(x=Avg_days_since_created,
y=Avg_days_since_pushed, color=IssuesF)) +
geom_point(shape=1) +    # Use hollow circles
geom_smooth()
ggsave(file="scatter-plot3.png", dpi=500)
```

We get the following output:

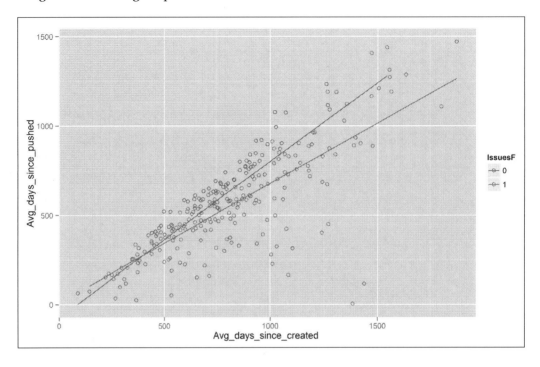

From the preceding scatter plot, we can see that there is a slight difference between the users with lesser issues and those with more issues. These are the different representations in the scatter plot; we can also see how each one of them is different and the value addition it brings in while interpreting the results. Also, the correlation function we used actually computes the correlation co-efficient using the default technique, the Pearson correlation. Alternatively, we can also try other correlation techniques such as Spearman and Kendall. It is advisable to read about which correlation technique is suitable for a particular dataset.

Correlation between the languages that user's use to code

In this section, we will answer just one question: *given a programmer programs in one language, what would be the other languages that they might know to code?*

In order to answer the preceding question, we need only the username and the languages the user had coded, from the master dataset. We can get that information by selecting the columns `full_name` and `language`:

```
ldata<- ausersubset[c("full_name","language")]
```

To find the correlation between the languages that the user's code in, we need to transpose the data. But in order to transpose the data, we need to format the datatype to data table using the R function `data.table`. Then, we can pivot the data using the function `dcast.data.table`, which comes along with the package `data.table`. Thus, we can convert the data to a required format:

```
library(data.table)
pivoting<- data.table(ldata)
pivotdata<-dcast.data.table(pivoting, full_name ~ language,
fun.aggregate=length, value.var="language")
```

We can find the correlation between the different languages using the `cor` function. The `cor` function would result in a matrix that will have correlation values between different languages. It will be complex to identify the combination that yields greater correlation; hence, we will again have to format the data to make our study easier:

```
ncol(pivotdata)
head(pivotdata)
pivotdata<- as.data.frame(pivotdata)
pivotdata<- pivotdata[,2:70]
cormatrix<- cor(pivotdata)
```

We will format the data using the following code, where we first remove the data in the diagonal, which is nothing but a self-correlation and will be always equal to 1. Then, we will remove the data in the upper diagonal as that is the redundant data. Finally, we will flatten the data into a table format using the function `melt`, which comes with the package `reshape`. Thus, we transformed the correlation data into an easily readable format. Now, we can filter the data based on a cut-off. It is the combination of languages that most likely comes together, which means if a user knows one of those languages, then it is most likely that they will know the other language in the combination. The code is as follows:

```
diag(cormatrix) <- NA
cormatrix[upper.tri (cormatrix)] <- NA
finalcor<- melt(cormatrix)
head(finalcor)
filteredcordata<- finalcor[ which(finalcor$value> 0.4),]
filteredcordata
```

We get the following output:

```
> filteredcordata
            Var1        Var2     value
4       ApacheConf       <NA> 0.4980870
135     TypeScript ActionScript 0.6234449
157            Coq       Agda 0.4960474
380           HaXe    Arduino 0.4291291
512             Go   Assembly 0.4392629
635            C++  AutoHotkey 0.4145410
756     TypeScript  Batchfile 0.4047566
879     PowerShell         C# 0.4994814
1275       Haskell        Coq 0.5657372
2756           TeX      Julia 0.4438608
2803      Makefile  LiveScript 0.4436783
2875    MoonScript        Lua 0.8919895
3099         Swift    Mercury 0.4884314
3237         Swift Objective-C 0.6130211
3518           XML  PowerShell 0.7057135
3782         Rebol          R 0.7638584
3791           TeX          R 0.6266375
3860           TeX      Rebol 0.4438608
> |
```

The preceding output is the solution to the question that we framed in the beginning of the chapter. In the preceding output, the pair `MoonScript` and `Lua` has the highest correlation.

How to get the trend of correlation?

So far, we have explored the correlation between different parameters and plotted the same in the scatter plot to visualize the relationship. Now, let's explore a methodology to find the trend in the correlation. We will check how the correlation between different parameters is affected by time. The rolling correlation will help us understand the volatility in the relationship between the parameters.

To solve this problem, let's consider the two parameters `watchers_count` and `forks_count`. First, we need to extract the data from the master dataset. We will use the following code to select those columns by their names:

```
mdata<- ausersubset[c("created_at", "watchers_count",
"forks_count")]
```

After extracting the data, we need to convert the column `created_at`, which is in the date-time format, to the date format supported by R using the function `as.POSIXct`. Also, we need to convert the other two columns to the numeric format so that we can perform aggregation at a daily level based on the date column and then find correlation between the two numeric columns. The code is as follows:

```
mdata$created_at<- as.POSIXct(strptime(mdata$created_at,
"%Y-%m-%d"))
```

```
mdata$watchers_count<- as.numeric(mdata$watchers_count)
mdata$forks_count<- as.numeric(mdata$forks_count)
```

Now we have the required data, but before going ahead with the correlation, we need to remove the duplicate rows by grouping the data on a date basis. To accomplish this, we need to use the package `data.table`, to convert the data into data table format and then we will perform the aggregation as mentioned using the following code. After the aggregation, we convert the data into the data frame format using the function `as.data.frame`. At last, we will use the function `merge` to get the data in the required format. The code is as follows:

```
library(data.table)
DT <- data.table(mdata)
m1 <- DT[, sum(forks_count ), by = created_at]
m2 <- DT[, sum(watchers_count ), by = created_at]
m1 <- as.data.frame(m1)
m2 <- as.data.frame(m2)
mdata<- merge(m1, m2, by = "created_at")
colnames(mdata) <- c("Date", "forks", "watchers")
```

Instead of performing the correlation on the complete set of historic data, we will select the latest 300 days of data using the function `tail`, since the data is in ascending order based on the date column. We will then make the date column a row name, and remove the date column. The code is as follows:

```
mdata1 <- tail(mdata, 300)
rownames(mdata1) <- mdata1$Date
mdata1 <- mdata1[,-1]
```

We will perform the rolling correlation using the `rollapplyr` function, which belongs to the package `zoo` and pass the parameter moving range set at 30 days. The computed correlation is saved to the data frame `r1`. We will then attach the actual date column to the correlation dataset by executing the following series of codes:

```
Library(zoo)
r1 <- rollapplyr(mdata1, 30, function(x) cor(x[,1],x[,2]),
by.column=FALSE)
r1 <- as.data.frame(r1)
r0 <- tail(mdata$Date, 271)
r0 <- as.data.frame(r0)
resultcor<- cbind(r0,r1)
colnames(resultcor) <- c("Date","Corr")
```

The data frame `resultcor` will actually hold the rolling correlation for the entire time period. But for visualization purposes, we will consider only the latest 75 days of data for plotting:

```
resultcor<- tail(resultcor, 75)
```

All of the preceding code is of no use if we don't add the visualization layer to the analysis. Hence, we will plot the trend of the correlation between the parameters `watchers_count` and `forks_count` using the function `ggplot` and save the plot using the `ggsave` function. In the following code, the parameter `geom_point()` is used to highlight the data points with a dot, and the parameter `geom_line()` is used for joining the dots with a line:

```
q <- ggplot(data=resultcor, aes(x=Date, y=Corr, group=1)) +
geom_line() + geom_point()
q + theme(axis.text.x = element_text(angle = 90, hjust = 1))
ggsave(file="C:/Users/Sharan/Desktop/SMM/Chapter 5/Pics/
roll-corr.png", dpi=500)
```

We get the following output:

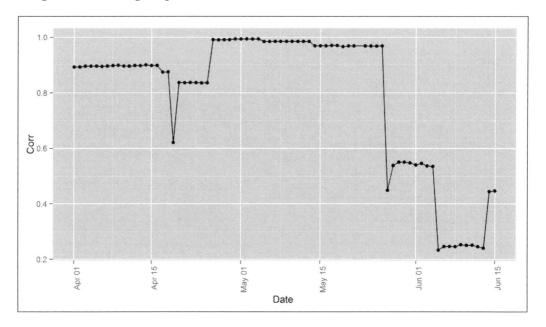

From the preceding output, we can see that the correlation between `watchers_count` and `forks_count` was very high until a few weeks back, but then in recent times the correlation has reached a minimum. In the preceding case, the low correlation in the recent data could be because of the lack of sufficient data or any other factor, for example, maybe these are very new repositories and it takes time to acquire `Watchers` or `Forks`. But, we successfully achieved our objective of exploring the data with different methods.

Note that EDA is the most important step in the process of data analysis; it is absolutely necessary to spend quality time in EDA as it will help in the following ways:

- It ensures better understanding of the data
- It allows us to test various hypotheses
- It allows us to uncover important insights from the data
- It allows us to detect anomalies
- It allows us to improve the accuracy of the predictive model based on the inputs from the EDA study

Reference

- For improvisation of the chart appearance, you can refer to the following links:

  ○ http://www.cookbook-r.com/Graphs/

  ○ http://www.statmethods.net/advgraphs/ggplot2.html

  ○ http://cran.r-project.org/web/packages/ggplot2/index.html

  ○ http://www.r-bloggers.com/search/ggplot2

- For more information on the GitHub package in R and the GitHub API, visit the following links:

  ○ https://github.com/cscheid/rgithub

  ○ https://developer.github.com/v3/

- Online courses on EDA can be found at:

  ○ https://www.coursera.org/course/exdata

  ○ https://www.udacity.com/course/data-analysis-with-r--ud651

Exercise

- Identify the set of parameters that have the most dynamic relationship in the last year.
- Choose any one parameter, aggregate on a daily level, and then plot the heat map to visualize the pattern across time.
- Try the scatter plot with the linear regression line and confidence interval of 75 percent.
- Identify the most popular repository as well as the most popular user.
- Instead of a moving correlation, perform correlation on a weekly and monthly basis. (Note that data will not be in moving range; it will be mutually exclusive.)

Business cases

Some of the business cases that can be implemented using the GitHub data are as follows:

- Identify the popular programmers in different languages.
- The online courses' websites can target potential subscribers based on suitable patterns in behavior.
- Provide recommendations to users on which user to follow as well as which repository to look out for.
- Identify the best people to target for a new open source project development in Java.
- Plot the trend on languages; here, the data point will be the number of repositories in a language. In order to get the trend, we need to pull the data on a daily basis to know how many new repositories are created and which language is used to develop them. This will help in understanding the lifecycle of language popularity.
- Build a regression model to predict the number of watchers a repository would get within a month of launch.

Summary

In this chapter, we covered the steps involved in the creation of the app on GitHub as well as the procedure for the installation and authentication using the GitHub package for R. We also discussed the public data that can be accessed using the GitHub API from R, implementation of some graphical and nongraphical EDA techniques on the GitHub data, and how to perform, as well as, interpret the correlation analysis.

By implementing the various EDA techniques and exploring the questions that were answered using it, we get a better understanding of when to use what kind of techniques for easier communication.

In the next chapter we will explore APIs of a few more social media sites such as LinkedIn, Tumblr, Wikipedia, Google Maps, Blogger, Foursquare and Quora. We will also cover use-cases that can be implemented.

6
More Social Media Websites

So far, we have discussed how to use the APIs of Twitter, Facebook, Instagram, and GitHub to make use of vital concepts and some machine learning techniques/ algorithms to answer critical business questions. In this chapter, we will see APIs of other social media websites, the methodology involved to pull data, the analysis that can be implemented, and cover some critical problems that can be solved.

Social media data is generally massive, noisy, and dynamic in nature; hence, taming data and performing the data analysis becomes challenging, but with a good grasp on the concepts it will be an amazing journey. With such huge data, they become rich sources of information that can help in various research fields and the business world.

The objective of this chapter is to understand the methodology involved in accessing data from social media websites, understanding the huge scope that social data analysis uncovers, as well as highlights on business cases that could be solved and the limitations involved.

The topics that will be covered in this chapter are as follows:

- Searching on social media
- Accessing product reviews from sites
- Retrieving data from Wikipedia
- Using the Tumblr API
- Accessing data from Quora
- Mapping solutions using Google Maps
- Professional network data using LinkedIn
- Getting Blogger data
- Retrieving venue data from Foursquare
- Yelp and other networks

Searching on social media

We will discuss how to use the package SocialMediaMineR in R, which would allow us to consider a few URLs and learn about the reach of those URLs in various social media websites. This package can get us details such as number of likes, shares, and comments on social media websites such as Facebook, Twitter, LinkedIn, Pinterest, reddit, and a few others. This package also has functions for pulling data specific to individual social networking sites.

We need to install the package and load it to the R environment, which can be done using the following code:

```
install.packages("SocialMediaMineR")
library(SocialMediaMineR)
```

After loading the package using the function library, we will proceed with using the various functions of the package. Let's start with the function get_facebook. This function will search for the mentioned URL in the social networking site Facebook, and it will return the mentioned URL; the normalized URL; and the number of Facebook shares, likes, comments, total hits, and clicks. This function can take input as any URL, normalize the URL, and then retrieve the details. The code is as follows:

```
get_facebook("http://www.bbc.com/")
```

We get the following output:

```
> fbresults
               url       normalized_url share_count like_count comment_count total_count
1 http://www.bbc.com/ http://www.bbc.com/     171627     120839         64653      357119
  click_count     comments_fbid commentsbox_count
1        7571 10150177473930506                 5
```

The get_pinterest function will give us the number of pins on Pinterest for the mentioned URL. This function can take any URL as input—blogs, YouTube videos shared, marketing campaigns, and so on. The code is as follows:

```
get_pinterest("http://www.bbc.com/")
```

We get the following output:

```
url count
1 http://www.bbc.com/  1281
```

We can perform analysis such as correlation on performance across different sites, trend analysis to decode the seasonality, reach to the audience, and much more on the preceding dataset.

The other site-specific functions that are part of the package `SocialMediaMineR` are `get_reddit`, `get_stumbleupon` and `get_twitter`. The function `get_reddit` will return a data frame associated with the performance of the URL on reddit, the function `get_stumbleupon` will give us the number of views on the website, the `stumbleupon` variable and the function `get_twitter` will return the count of number of tweets. Here's the code for `get_reddit`:

```
get_reddit("http://www.bbc.com/")
```

We get the following output:

```
> get_reddit("http://www.bbc.com/")
  domain banned_by subreddit selftext_html selftext likes secure_media link_flair_text
1 bbc.com        NA      news            NA       NA    NA           NA              NA
      id gilded clicked stickied    author media score approved_by over_18 hidden
1 2wjf57      0   FALSE    FALSE lisalondon    NA     1          NA   FALSE  FALSE
  thumbnail subreddit_id edited link_flair_css_class author_flair_css_class downs saved
1                t5_2qh31  FALSE                   NA                     NA     0 FALSE
  is_self                  permalink      name   created                     url
1   FALSE /r/news/comments/2wjf57/bbc/ t3_2wjf57 1424433155 http://www.bbc.com/
  author_flair_text title created_utc distinguished num_comments visited num_reports ups
1                NA   BBC  1424433155            NA            0   FALSE          NA   1
```

Here's the code for `get_stumbleupon`:

```
get_stumbleupon("http://www.bbc.com/")
```

We get the following output:

```
> get_stumbleupon("http://www.bbc.com/")
        result.url result.in_index result.publicid result.views    result.title
1 http://bbc.com/             TRUE          1cMT38          123 BBC - Homepage
                               result.thumbnail
1 http://cdn.stumble-upon.com/mthumb/329/895329.jpg
                             result.thumbnail_b
1 http://cdn.stumble-upon.com/bthumb/329/895329.jpg
                               result.submit_link
1 http://www.stumbleupon.com/badge/?url=http://bbc.com/
                                result.badge_link
1 http://www.stumbleupon.com/badge/?url=http://bbc.com/
                        result.info_link   timestamp success
1 http://www.stumbleupon.com/url/bbc.com/ 1438451988    TRUE
```

Here's the code for `get_twitter`:

```
get_twitter("http://www.bbc.com/")
```

We get the following output:

```
counturl
1 585637 http://www.bbc.com/
```

If there is access only to the shortened URL, then we can use the following function to retrieve the actual URL so that we can use it in any of the preceding functions:

```
get_url("http://goo.gl/muN6lV")
```

We get the following output:

```
                    http://goo.gl/muN6lV
"http://www.rsharankumar.com/"
```

Now, we will see the `get_socialmedia` function of the `SocialMediaMineR` package. This function will return the popularity of the URL from multiple social networking websites. This function can take multiple URLs as input, so we first hold a few sets of news channel URLs in the variable `news_urls`. In the following example, we will compare the performance of different news channel websites in social networking websites:

```
news_urls<- c(
  "http://www.bbc.com/",
  "http://www.euronews.com/",
  "http://www.cnn.com/",
  "http://www.nytimes.com/",
  "http://www.guardian.co.uk/",
  "http://www.globalpost.com/",
  "http://www.france24.com/",
  "http://www.aljazeera.com/",
  "http://www.reuters.com/",
  "http://www.foxnews.com/",
  "http://www.nbcnews.com/",
  "http://www.huffingtonpost.com/",
  "http://www.wsj.com/",
  "http://www.ndtv.com/")
```

We use the function `get_socialmedia` and pass the variable that holds all these URLs as an input parameter. The optional parameter `sleep.time` is used to specify the number of seconds the function should wait before proceeding to the next URL. This will be very useful in case there are multiple URLs and we don't want to reach the API call limit. For the preceding URLs, we have got the popularity metrics across different websites. The code is as follows:

```
allresults<- get_socialmedia(news_urls, sleep.time = 0)
allresults
```

Note that the preceding function might throw some errors, but most likely the right result will be generated.

We get the following output:

```
> allresults
                           url                  normalized_url fbk_shares fbk_likes fbk_comments fbk_total
1             http://www.bbc.com/             http://www.bbc.com/     171627    120839        64653    357119
2        http://www.euronews.com/        http://www.euronews.com/      12771      5871         1906     20548
3             http://www.cnn.com/             http://www.cnn.com/     478271    684519       157865   1320655
4         http://www.nytimes.com/         http://www.nytimes.com/     317849    252538        94082    664469
5      http://www.guardian.co.uk/      http://www.guardian.co.uk/        464       686          423      1573
6       http://www.globalpost.com/      http://www.globalpost.com/       1243       539          433      2215
7         http://www.france24.com/         http://www.france24.com/     25077     26415        10040     61532
8        http://www.aljazeera.com/        http://www.aljazeera.com/      1545      1749          698      3992
9          http://www.reuters.com/          http://www.reuters.com/     22890      9747         7021     39658
10         http://www.foxnews.com/         http://www.foxnews.com/     119292    120634        72778    312704
11         http://www.nbcnews.com/         http://www.nbcnews.com/      75463     40457        31550    147470
12 http://www.huffingtonpost.com/ http://www.huffingtonpost.com/     156657    104087        63456    324200
13             http://www.wsj.com/             http://www.wsj.com/       9789      4677         1809     16275
14            http://www.ndtv.com/            http://www.ndtv.com/      12300      7022         1236     20558
   fbk_clicks twt_tweets rdt_score rdt_downs rdt_ups rdt_comments lkn_shares stu_views pin_counts
1        7571     585637         1         0       1            0         NA       123       1281
2           0      12937        26         0      26            3         NA       136         17
3           0    9837943        39         0      39           25         NA     26365       9495
4        5353    2788792         0         0       0            6         NA    285429      21280
5           0     193790         1         0       1            0         NA     44616       9787
6          17       1883         0         0       0            0         NA      1747         31
7         132         13        NA        NA      NA           NA         NA        10          0
8           0     197256         1         0       1            0         NA       392        297
9           0     460708         9         0       9            3         NA     48472        247
10       3103     400966         3         0       3            0         NA     10027      13616
11          0    1180847       183         0     183           31         NA       402      13515
12        515     296312         1         0       1            0         NA    119398      28556
13       3266      83413         5         0       5            1         NA        13        313
14          0      79042         5         0       5            0         NA       157         28
```

The `SocialMediaMineR` package will be very useful to identify the performance of a list of blogs, brands, and businesses. It will be a convenient way to measure the performance across multiple online sites. Please note that the data generated by each of the preceding functions is very different in each case, as the data format depends on the availability and accessibility provided by the social media sites.

Exercise

Consider the English Premier League, create a list of websites of your favorite teams, and evaluate their performance in social networking websites. Check out which team had the maximum penetration in social media.

Accessing product reviews from sites

Online product reviews are a very good source of information. They can be used to judge a brand or a product. It becomes very difficult to read all the reviews, so we can write a program to get the product reviews. Let's see one of the ways to extract the customer review data from Amazon. For example, let's consider the movie *Transformers – Age of Extinction* and see the customer reviews:

```
url1<-
'http://www.amazon.com/gp/video/detail/B00L83TQR6?ie=UTF8&redirect
=true&ref_=s9_nwrsa_gw_g318_i1'
```

First, we get the relevant URL and store it in a variable so that it can be used in the functions. Then, we need to parse the HTML content of the page and save it to the variable doc. In order to do so, we need to import the package XML. Now, the parsed HTML is stored in the variable doc. Please follow the link for more details on the HTML DOM: http://www.w3schools.com/jsref/dom_obj_document.asp. The code is as follows:

```
library(XML)
doc<- htmlParse(url1)
```

From this parsed data, we can get the required information by specifying the class in which the content is present, using the function xpathSApply. In our case, the customer reviews are present in the tag div with the class name a-section. The following code will extract the customer reviews.

```
review<- xpathSApply(doc,'//div[@class="a-section"]',xmlValue)
data.frame(review)
```

> Note that the websites, in the preceding case Amazon, might change the DOM structure. Hence, verify the DOM structure before executing the preceding code. Also, note that this data would require processing before consumption in the analysis.

We get the following output:

```
                                                                    \n  I love all
the transformers movies, just because they're entertaining.  I know they're not critical
ly acclaimed for the acting or the heart-wrenching story like say a Terms of Endearment,
 but they're not supposed to be.  They're action, they're visually spectacular, and very
 fun!  It's escapism at it's best.  watching these movies with a nice surround system is
 a must.  The explosions, the sounds of the transforming, all of it is a much better exp
erience with surround and a good subwoofer!  I can do without 2 things in the movies...t
he eye candy that is the chicks in short shorts!  To me, it just doesn't add to the movi
e.  I guess because I'm not a adolescent teenage boy.  Secondly, is the language.  it se
ems like all sequels, things are pushed further each time another one is made.  There wa
s more profanity in this one than the others.  It too doesn't add to the movie.  My 4 ye
ar old son loves Transformers, too and I don't want him picking up the language.  I know
 one day he will be exposed to it, but c'mon!  These movies are enjoyed by all age group
s,  Michael Bay, please tone down those 2 things and all will be well.  Mark wahlberg di
d a good job in the movie... I like his movies anyway.  I didn't miss Shia LaBeouf or an
y of the other actors from the previous ones.  Also, this one had more work done on the
video side.  The greens were way greener.  My wife noticed that almost everyone had colo
red eyes, and over exaggerated at that.  I didn't mind all that, but it did seem a littl
e weird.  I loved the robots!  All of them were too cool...Lockdown is a bad dude!  His
walk, his whole demeanor...I found myself liking him.  Those Dinobots were massive!  I c
an't wait to watch it again...and for the next one, which is probably already in the wor
ks.\n
5
```

 The preceding output is just a part of the actual output.

This customer feedback is a rich source of information, and it can be used for a variety of use cases. Brands can monitor their product performance across different geographic locations. It can also be used for product enhancement.

The logic discussed here can be used to parse the data from any website. Hence, the use cases are not only limited to ecommerce reviews, it can also be used in cases where the data is present in the form of websites.

Retrieving data from Wikipedia

Wikipedia is an open source encyclopedia project developed collaboratively by multiple people across the world. This is a rich source of information, and we can find content about anything in this world. In this section, we are going to check out the ways to extract the content from Wikipedia for our analysis. We will concentrate only on the tabular content.

We will consider the Wikipedia page on *List of countries and dependencies by population*. This page has tabular content about the countries and their population. This is shown in the following screenshot:

Countries and dependencies by population [edit]

Note: All dependent territories or countries that are parts of sovereign states are shown in *italics*.

Rank ‡	Country (or dependent territory) ‡	Population ‡	Date ‡	% of world population ‡	Source
1	China[Note 2]	1,371,300,000	August 3, 2015	18.9%	Official population clock ☞
2	India	1,275,070,000	August 3, 2015	17.6%	Official population clock ☞
3	United States	321,537,000	August 3, 2015	4.43%	Official population clock ☞
4	Indonesia	255,770,000	July 1, 2015	3.52%	Official projection ☞
5	Brazil	204,695,000	August 3, 2015	2.82%	Official population clock ☞
6	Pakistan	190,521,000	August 3, 2015	2.62%	Official population clock ☞
7	Nigeria	182,202,000	July 1, 2015	2.53%	UN projection ☞
8	Bangladesh	158,785,000	August 3, 2015	2.19%	Official population clock ☞
9	Russia[Note 3]	146,539,530	August 3, 2015	2.02%	Official population clock ☞
10	Japan	126,865,000	July 1, 2015	1.75%	Monthly official estimate ☞

Now, we will see how to bring the preceding tabular content to R so that we can perform some computation. Before going into the coding, you have to understand that the method explored is just one way of implementing it. This can be performed in multiple ways.

For the method we are discussing, we need to load the package `httr` and then read the URL of the mentioned Wikipedia page. We need to pass the URL to the function GET. The GET method will retrieve the data identified by the requested URL. If the URL refers to the data producing process, then the data that will be produced will be returned and not the actual text content at source. Then, we pass on the content to `tabs`. The function `readHTMLTable` is a robust method of extracting the data from the tables in HTML documents. This function will read all the tables present in the specified URL. Also, this function attempts to perform heuristic computation to get the headers for the columns. The code is as follows:

```
library(httr)
url1 <-
"https://en.wikipedia.org/wiki/
List_of_countries_and_dependencies_by_population"
tabs<- GET(url1)
tabs<-
readHTMLTable(rawToChar(tabs$content), stringsAsFactors = F)
```

Now, all the tabular data is copied to `tabs`. This content will be of the type `list`. Browse through the list that has been extracted; you will find that the first list contains the actual table. Hence, we filter out the first table data and leave the other data:

```
class(tabs)
```

We get the following output:

```
[1] "list"
```

We use the following code to extract the table content alone from the preceding list.

```
tablecontent<- tabs$'NULL'
head(tablecontent)
```

We get the following output:

```
> head(tablecontent, 10)
   Rank Country (or dependent territory)    Population          Date
1   1                     China[Note 2] 1,371,300,000 August 3, 2015
2   2                             India 1,275,070,000 August 3, 2015
3   3                     United States   321,537,000 August 3, 2015
4   4                         Indonesia   255,770,000    July 1, 2015
5   5                            Brazil   204,695,000 August 3, 2015
6   6                          Pakistan   190,521,000 August 3, 2015
7   7                           Nigeria   182,202,000    July 1, 2015
8   8                        Bangladesh   158,785,000 August 3, 2015
9   9                    Russia[Note 3]   146,539,530 August 3, 2015
10  10                            Japan   126,865,000    July 1, 2015
   % of world\npopulation                 Source
1                  18.9% Official population clock
2                  17.6% Official population clock
3                  4.43% Official population clock
4                  3.52%        Official projection
5                  2.82% Official population clock
6                  2.62% Official population clock
7                  2.53%              UN projection
8                  2.19% Official population clock
9                  2.02% Official population clock
10                 1.75% Monthly official estimate
```

The same function and methods can be used for multiple purposes. We can read any Wikipedia page that has content in a table. This data can now be used for any visualization/exploratory analysis.

Apart from the method discussed here, there are other ways to retrieve data. Instead of using the function `GET`, we can also use the function `getURL`. However, this function also needs to load the package `RCurl`.

Now that we know how to download tabular content from Wikipedia, we will explore ways of getting the details on the Wikipedia users who contributed to the content, the difference between the revisions made to a page, and more. Let's review some of it.

In order to retrieve the preceding details, we use the package `WikipediR`. Download the latest package from GitHub. First load the package `devtools`, and then install the package `WikipediR` using the function `install_github` to make sure that the latest package is downloaded:

```
install.packages("Rtools")
library(devtools)
install_github("Ironholds/WikipediR")
library(WikipediR)
```

We can get the text content of various pages in Wikipedia. First, let's see how to get the text content from a random page. We can get this using the function `random_page`. Every time we run the function, we would get the data of a new page in Wikipedia. The content extracted is of the type `pcontent`, it is a parsed text. The code is as follows:

```
randomContent<- random_page("en","wikipedia")
head(randomContent)
```

We get the following output:

```
> head(randomContent)
$parse
$parse$title
[1] "Anwar Hamed"

$parse$revid
[1] 607840000

$parse$text
$parse$text$`*`
[1] "<p><b>Anwar Hamed</b> (born 1957) is a <a href=\"/wiki/Palestinian_people\" title=\
"Palestinian people\" class=\"mw-redirect\">Palestinian</a>-<a href=\"/wiki/Hungary\" ti
tle=\"Hungary\">Hungarian</a> novelist, poet and author.<sup id=\"cite_ref-1\" class=\"r
eference\"><a href=\"#cite_note-1\"><span>[</span>1<span>]</span></a></sup> He was born
in the <a href=\"/wiki/West_Bank\" title=\"West Bank\">West Bank</a> and went to Hungary
 for college. His first short stories were published in <a href=\"/wiki/Arabic\" title=\
"Arabic\">Arabic</a> when he was still a teenager in the West Bank, but after his move t
o Hungary, he started writing in Hungarian. His first novels were written in this langua
ge. Since 2004, he has been living in London, where he works for <a href=\"/wiki/BBC_Ara
bic\" title=\"BBC Arabic\">BBC Arabic</a>.<sup id=\"cite_ref-2\" class=\"reference\"><a
href=\"#cite_note-2\"><span>[</span>2<span>]</span></a></sup></p>\n<p>His novel <i>Jaffa
 Prepares Morning Coffee</i> was longlisted for the 2013 <a href=\"/wiki/Arabic_Booker_P
rize\" title=\"Arabic Booker Prize\" class=\"mw-redirect\">Arabic Booker Prize</a>. </p>\
n<h2><span class=\"mw-headline\" id=\"Selected_works\">Selected works</span><span class=
\"mw-editsection\"><span class=\"mw-editsection-bracket\">[</span><a href=\"/w/index.php
?title=Anwar_Hamed&amp;action=edit&amp;section=1\" title=\"Edit section: Selected works\
">edit</a><span class=\"mw-editsection-bracket\">]</span></span></h2>\n<ul>\n<li><i>The
Bridge of Babylon</i></li>\n<li><i>Stones of Pain</i></li>\n<li><i>Scheherazade Tells Ta
les No More</i></li>\n<li><i>The Game of Love and Pride and Other Idiocies</i></li>\n<li
><i>Valse Triste</i></li>\n<li><i>Seventy-Two Virgins and a Confused Lad</i></li>\n<li><
i>Jaffa Prepares Morning Coffee</i></li>\n<li>Jenin 2002</li>\n<li><i>Mind the Gap</i> (
poetry)</li>\n<li><i>Oh, Those Days!</i> (short stories)</li>\n<li><i>Literary theory: A
n attempt towards the definition of the function of literature</i> (theory)</li>\n</ul>\
n<h2><span class=\"mw-headline\" id=\"References\">References</span><span class=\"mw-edi
tsection\"><span class=\"mw-editsection-bracket\">[</span><a href=\"/w/index.php?title=A
nwar_Hamed&amp;action=edit&amp;section=2\" title=\"Edit section: References\">edit</a><s
```

This output is just a screenshot of the actual output.

We will now see how to extract the text from a specific page on Wikipedia. We can do this using the function `page_content` and extract the contents from a specific Wikipedia page. Here's the code to extract the contents from the page about *Dr. A.P.J. Abdul Kalam*:

```
pageContent<- page_content("en","wikipedia",
page_name = "A._P._J._Abdul_Kalam")
head(pageContent)
```

We get the following output:

```
> head(pageContent)
$parse
$parse$title
[1] "A. P. J. Abdul Kalam"

$parse$revid
[1] 674484862

$parse$text
$parse$text$`*`
[1] "<div class=\"hatnote\">This article is about the former President of India.  For th
e Indian freedom fighter, see <a href=\"/wiki/Abul_Kalam_Azad\" title=\"Abul Kalam Azad\
">Abul Kalam Azad</a>.</div>\n<table class=\"infobox vcard\" style=\"width: 22em;\">\n<t
r>\n<th colspan=\"2\" class=\"n\" style=\"text-align: center; font-size: 132%;\">\n<span c
lass=\"fn\">ஆ. ப. ஜெ. அப்துல் கலாம்<br />nA. P. J. Abdul Kalam</span><br />\n<span clas
s=\"honorific-suffix\" style=\"font-size:76%; font-weight:normal;\"><small style=\"font-
size:85%;\"><a href=\"/wiki/Bharat_Ratna\" title=\"Bharat Ratna\">Bharat Ratna</a></smal
l></span></th>\n</tr>\n<tr>\n<td colspan=\"2\" style=\"text-align: center\"><a href=\"/w
iki/File:Apj_abdul_kalam.JPG\" class=\"image\"><img alt=\"Apj abdul kalam.JPG\" src=\"//
upload.wikimedia.org/wikipedia/commons/thumb/3/34/Apj_abdul_kalam.JPG/230px-Apj_abdul_ka
lam.JPG\" width=\"230\" height=\"274\" srcset=\"//upload.wikimedia.org/wikipedia/commons
/thumb/3/34/Apj_abdul_kalam.JPG/345px-Apj_abdul_kalam.JPG 1.5x, //upload.wikimedia.org/w
ikipedia/commons/thumb/3/34/Apj_abdul_kalam.JPG/460px-Apj_abdul_kalam.JPG 2x\" data-file
-width=\"644\" data-file-height=\"768\" /></a></td>\n</tr>\n<tr>\n<td colspan=\"2\" styl
e=\"text-align: center\">Kalam at the International Book Fair, Trivandrum, 2014</td>\n</
tr>\n<tr>\n<th colspan=\"2\" style=\"background-color: lavender; text-align: center\"><a
 href=\"/wiki/List_of_Presidents_of_India\" title=\"List of Presidents of India\">11th</
a> <a href=\"/wiki/President_of_India\" title=\"President of India\">President of India<
/a></th>\n</tr>\n<tr>\n<td colspan=\"2\" style=\"border-bottom:none; text-align:center\"
><span class=\"nowrap\"><b>In office</b></span><br />\n25 July 2002 - 25 July 2007<
/td>\n</tr>\n<tr>\n<th style=\"text-align:left;\"><span class=\"nowrap\">Prime Minister<
/span></th>\n<td><a href=\"/wiki/Atal_Bihari_Vajpayee\" title=\"Atal Bihari Vajpayee\">A
tal Bihari Vajpayee</a><br />\n<a href=\"/wiki/Manmohan_Singh\" title=\"Manmohan Singh\"
>Manmohan Singh</a></td>\n</tr>\n<tr>\n<th style=\"text-align:left;\"><span class=\"nowr
ap\">Vice President</span></th>\n<td><a href=\"/wiki/Krishan_Kant\" title=\"Krishan Kant
\">Krishan Kant</a><br />\n<a href=\"/wiki/Bhairon_Singh_Shekhawat\" title=\"Bhairon Sin
gh Shekhawat\">Bhairon Singh Shekhawat</a></td>\n</tr>\n<tr>\n<th style=\"text-align:lef
```

This output is just a screenshot of the actual output.

We can get to know about the revisions made to the Wikipedia page using the function `revision_diff`; we need to pass the page ID in order to get the revision details. The following code generates the revision details for the page titled *A.P.J. Abdul_Kalam*:

```
revision_diff("en","wikipedia", revisions = 674484862,
direction = "next")
```

We get the following output:

```
> revision_diff("en","wikipedia", revisions = 674484862, direction = "next")
$batchcomplete
[1] ""

$query
$query$pages
$query$pages$`62682`
$query$pages$`62682`$pageid
[1] 62682

$query$pages$`62682`$ns
[1] 0

$query$pages$`62682`$title
[1] "A. P. J. Abdul Kalam"

$query$pages$`62682`$revisions
$query$pages$`62682`$revisions[[1]]
$query$pages$`62682`$revisions[[1]]$revid
[1] 674484862

$query$pages$`62682`$revisions[[1]]$parentid
[1] 674460628
```

 This output is just a screenshot of the actual output.

The package `WikipediR` allows us to extract the backlinks. In the following code, we will extract the backlinks of the page `A._P._J._Abdul_Kalam`:

```
page_backlinks("en","wikipedia", page = "A._P._J._Abdul_Kalam")
```

We get the following output:

```
> page_backlinks("en","wikipedia", page = "A._P._J._Abdul_Kalam")
$warnings
$warnings$query
$warnings$query$`*`
[1] "Formatting of continuation data has changed. To receive raw query-continue data, us
e the 'rawcontinue' parameter. To silence this warning, pass an empty string for 'contin
ue' in the initial query."


$batchcomplete
[1] ""

$continue
$continue$blcontinue
[1] "0|49708"

$continue$continue
[1] "-||"


$query
$query$backlinks
$query$backlinks[[1]]
$query$backlinks[[1]]$pageid
[1] 14604

$query$backlinks[[1]]$ns
[1] 0

$query$backlinks[[1]]$title
[1] "Foreign relations of India"
```

 This output is just a screenshot of the actual output.

Now that we know how to extract and parse tabular content, let's see how to extract the details of the users who actually edited and worked on the various URLs. We can use the following code to extract the details on the contributions made as well as the general user information. The function `ucontribution` can be used to get the contribution made by a specific user. In the following case, we are retrieving only the timestamp of those contributions, but we can also get the comments for those contributions by replacing timestamp with comment:

```
user_contributions("en", "wikipedia",
username = "Ironholds", properties = "timestamp")
```

We get the following output:

```
$query
$query$usercontribs
$query$usercontribs[[1]]
$query$usercontribs[[1]]$userid
[1] 6804626

$query$usercontribs[[1]]$user
[1] "Ironholds"

$query$usercontribs[[1]]$timestamp
[1] "2015-08-04T07:19:13Z"


$query$usercontribs[[2]]
$query$usercontribs[[2]]$userid
[1] 6804626

$query$usercontribs[[2]]$user
[1] "Ironholds"

$query$usercontribs[[2]]$timestamp
[1] "2015-08-03T21:00:05Z"


$query$usercontribs[[3]]
$query$usercontribs[[3]]$userid
[1] 6804626

$query$usercontribs[[3]]$user
[1] "Ironholds"

$query$usercontribs[[3]]$timestamp
[1] "2015-08-03T20:59:35Z"
```

[This output is just a screenshot of the actual output.]

The function user_information gives us the basic information about the users. To the parameter properties, we pass all the information required to be captured. Here's the code to get the details of the user rsharankumar:

```
user_information("en", "wikipedia", user_names = "rsharankumar",
properties = c("blockinfo", "groups", "implicitgroups", "rights",
"editcount", "registration", "emailable", "gender"))
```

We get the following output:

```
$batchcomplete
[1] ""

$query
$query$users
$query$users[[1]]
$query$users[[1]]$userid
[1] 15168084

$query$users[[1]]$name
[1] "Rsharankumar"

$query$users[[1]]$editcount
[1] 0

$query$users[[1]]$registration
[1] "2011-08-19T05:38:15Z"

$query$users[[1]]$groups
$query$users[[1]]$groups[[1]]
[1] "*"

$query$users[[1]]$groups[[2]]
[1] "user"


$query$users[[1]]$implicitgroups
$query$users[[1]]$implicitgroups[[1]]
[1] "*"

$query$users[[1]]$implicitgroups[[2]]
[1] "user"


$query$users[[1]]$rights
$query$users[[1]]$rights[[1]]
```

This output is just a screenshot of the actual output.

The preceding dataset includes a lot of junk data as well, but by using the functions we discussed in the chapters so far, such as the fromJSON, GET, and as.data.frame, we can process the data and convert it to a consumable format. Here's a sample method that can be used to get the user details in the data frame format from the above dataset:

```
data <- user_information("en", "wikipedia", user_names =
"rsharankumar", properties = c("blockinfo", "groups",
"implicitgroups", "rights", "editcount", "registration",
"emailable", "gender"))
sample <- data$query$users[[1]]
sample <- as.data.frame(sample)
```

The objective of this book is to show you the art of getting the required data from different social media sites. Initially, we were using the URL of the various pages and were parsing the data to extract the required data. Later, we saw how to use the WikipediR package, which was built to communicate with Wikipedia and give us the required information. The latter is always preferable because of the effort that would have been needed to provide the data in a readable format. In the case of Wikipedia, authentication was not required to extract the data, but in most other cases it will be required to authenticate before extracting the data. Wikipedia has good information about various topics, so knowing how to access the data provides us a huge advantage.

Exercise

Since most country's pages in Wikipedia are similar to each other, we can write scripts to pull data about different countries and compare the difference. Similar analysis can be done across different domains.

You can find the list of top contributors from https://en.wikipedia.org/wiki/Wikipedia:List_of_Wikipedians_by_number_of_edits.

Identify if there is correlation between the users' contribution and the time they registered with Wikipedia. Also, try to get some information like the gender breakups and so on.

Using the Tumblr API

Tumblr is a microblogging and social networking platform. Tumblr, as of August 2015, hosts around 248 million blogs and about 117 billion posts, and over 75 million posts are created on a daily basis. In this section, we will see how to access the data from Tumblr and, in the process, understand how the steps involved are different from the methodology discussed so far.

There is a package in R that allows interaction with Tumblr. We need to install the package `tumblR`. The package has little dependency, so use the following code for installation:

```
install.packages("tumblR")
install.packages("base64enc")
install.packages("httpuv")
library(tumblR)
```

The preceding code installs the related packages, as well as loads the required package on to the working environment.

We need to have an account in Tumblr and have the app for enabling authentication in order to access the data. Once we create the app, we get the consumer key and the secret key. We can use these to access the data, or we can authenticate and save the details as a token and use just the token for data access. We can register for an app at `http://www.tumblr.com/oauth/apps`.

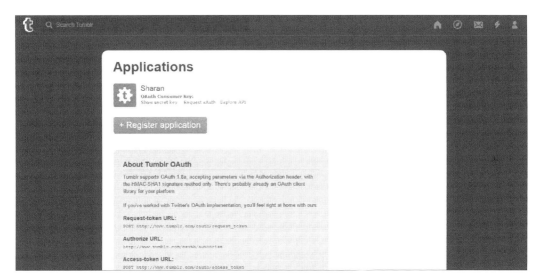

In order to authenticate, we need some more information such as the consumer key and the secret key. Hence, we save those to a variable so that we can simply use these variables instead of having to mention it in several places. The code is as follows:

```
consumer_key<-'Paste your key here'
consumer_secret<- 'Paste your secret key here'
appname<- 'Paste your App name here'
tokenURL<- 'http://www.tumblr.com/oauth/request_token'
accessTokenURL<- 'http://www.tumblr.com/oauth/access_token'
authorizeURL<- 'http://www.tumblr.com/oauth/authorize'
```

Now we will see how to use the preceding details to complete the authentication process. The first variable will hold the app details, the name, consumer key, and the consumer secret code and the variable `endpoint` holds the details about end points to hit. The code is as follows:

```
app<- oauth_app(appname, consumer_key, consumer_secret)
endpoint<- oauth_endpoint(tokenURL, authorizeURL, accessTokenURL)
token<- oauth1.0_token(endpoint, app)
```

The function `oauth1.0_token` uses the app details and the end point details to initiate the authentication. Similar to the action performed in Facebook and Instagram, the authentication function opens the browser on providing the user name and password. Approving the following message in the popup completes the authentication process:

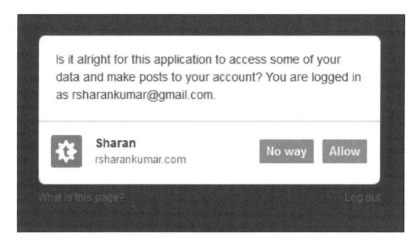

```
> token <- oauth1.0_token(endpoint, app)
Waiting for authentication in browser...
Press Esc/Ctrl + C to abort
Authentication complete.
```

We get a confirmation note in the R environment also. Now, the authentication process is completed and we can go ahead and access the data that is available. We can also get a few blogs present in Tumblr and start accessing the data. In this section, we will explore some of the functions and some of the use cases that could be implemented using the available data.

We will consider the `ifpaintingscouldtext.tumblr.com` blog in Tumblr and figure out the usage of a few functions belonging to the package `tumblR`. First, let's retrieve the avatar of the blog. The **avatar** is the visual representation or the profile picture used in the blog's profile. We can get the blog's avatar using the function `avatar`. The second parameter represents the size of the image. The code is as follows:

```
avatar(base_hostname = url, size =64)
```

We get the following output:

```
[1] "https://33.media.tumblr.com/avatar_e4ac5327294d_64.png"
```

In the output, we get the URL of the avatar of the blog. We can visit the mentioned URL to get the avatar of the mentioned blog. We can also get the details of a blog using the function `info.blog`:

```
info.blog(base_hostname = url, api_key = consumer_key)
```

Here's the output of the function. We get some basic information about the blog:

```
> info.blog(base_hostname = url, api_key = consumer_key)
$meta
$meta$status
[1] 200

$meta$msg
[1] "OK"


$response
$response$blog
$response$blog$title
[1] "If Paintings Could Text"

$response$blog$name
[1] "ifpaintingscouldtext"

$response$blog$posts
[1] 171

$response$blog$url
[1] "http://ifpaintingscouldtext.tumblr.com/"

$response$blog$updated
[1] 1438128071

$response$blog$description
[1] "A revival of classical art and epic texts."

$response$blog$is_nsfw
[1] FALSE

$response$blog$ask
[1] TRUE

$response$blog$ask_page_title
[1] "Ask "
```

We can get the post and the reposts that were liked in the blog. To get that, we need to use the function `likes`. This function retrieves the publicly exposed likes from a blog:

```
likes(base_hostname = url, limit = 20, offset = 0,
api_key = consumer_key)
```

Let's see the likes in the preceding blog.

```
$meta
$meta$status
[1] 200

$meta$msg
[1] "OK"


$response
$response$liked_posts
$response$liked_posts[[1]]
$response$liked_posts[[1]]$blog_name
[1] "classic-art"

$response$liked_posts[[1]]$id
[1] 1.11632e+11

$response$liked_posts[[1]]$post_url
[1] "http://classic-art.tumblr.com/post/111632000975/the-mirror-leo-whelan-1912"

$response$liked_posts[[1]]$slug
[1] "the-mirror-leo-whelan-1912"

$response$liked_posts[[1]]$type
[1] "photo"

$response$liked_posts[[1]]$date
[1] "2015-02-21 05:38:40 GMT"

$response$liked_posts[[1]]$timestamp
[1] 1424497120

$response$liked_posts[[1]]$state
[1] "published"

$response$liked_posts[[1]]$format
```

While this package allows us to retrieve the data from the blog, it also has a few functions that would allow us to update the blog of a particular user and also to perform certain action such as following a blog, liking a blog plot, and so on. In order to know more about the data that could be captured, visit https://cran.r-project.org/web/packages/tumblR/tumblR.pdf.

While the preceding package provides all of the specified functionalities, we can also make use of the alternative package, which has a similar name to get some additional data. Kindly note that the API from Tumblr, or for that matter any website, is subject to changes from time to time. Hence, there could be some functions in the packages that could be possibly deprecated. Try out the following code as well:

```
library(devtools)
install_github("klapaukh/tumblR")
setup_tumblr_apikey(consumer_secret)
all = get_posts("staff.tumblr.com")
posts = all$posts
head(posts)
```

We get the following output:

```
$posts[[20]]
$posts[[20]]$blog_name
[1] "staff"

$posts[[20]]$id
[1] 124694265970

$posts[[20]]$post_url
[1] "http://staff.tumblr.com/post/124694265970/derekeads-chill-by-derek-eads-this-air"

$posts[[20]]$slug
[1] "derekeads-chill-by-derek-eads-this-air"

$posts[[20]]$type
[1] "photo"

$posts[[20]]$date
[1] "2015-07-21 22:01:14 GMT"

$posts[[20]]$timestamp
[1] 1437516074

$posts[[20]]$state
[1] "published"

$posts[[20]]$format
[1] "html"

$posts[[20]]$reblog_key
[1] "cr6TiDnE"

$posts[[20]]$tags
$posts[[20]]$tags[[1]]
[1] "summer week"
```

To know more about the second package, visit `https://github.com/klapaukh/tumblR`.

Exercise:

Find out the most popular blogs on Tumblr, start collecting details about these blogs, and apply a clustering algorithm to figure out the blogs that are similar to each other. In the process, get the most popular blogs based on the likes and other factors, if any.

Accessing data from Quora

Quora is a popular question and answer website where questions are asked, answered, and managed by the community members and the entire operations is *gamified*. The interesting answers can get some points and the users could also shell out some points to get some of their questions answered by certain people.

There are ways to get the data from Quora, but there is an unofficial API which returns the data in the JSON format. It is actually a set of URLs that will provide us with the required information. These URLs will also work in browsers. Once we get the data in the JSON format, we can convert it into the data frame format later.

Let's see some of the URLs and ways to use it in R. The API's base URL is `http://quora.christopher.su`. To the base URL, we need to add the following to get the relevant data:

- `/users/<user>/activity/answers`
- `/users/<user>/activity/user_follows`
- `/users/<user>/activity/want_answers`
- `/users/<user>/activity/upvotes`
- `/users/<user>/activity/review_requests`

First, we will try to get the user's profile details. The following code will provide us with the details of the specified user in the JSON format. It provides some basic information like the followers, following, number of posts and the total number of edits made, questions asked, and the answers made:

```
udata<- fromJSON("http://quora.christopher.su/users/
Sharan-Kumar-R")
```

We get the following output:

```
> udata
$answers
[1] 7

$blogs
NULL

$edits
[1] 32

$followers
[1] 253

$following
[1] 204

$name
[1] "Sharan Kumar R"

$posts
[1] 3

$questions
[1] 0

$topics
NULL

$username
[1] "Sharan-Kumar-R"
```

Given that we know the questions in Quora, we can get to know about its category, as well as the number of answers it received. This can be done with the following code:

```
fromJSON("http://quora.christopher.su/questions/
If-space-is-3-dimensional-can-time-also-be-3-dimensional")
```

We get the following output:

```
> fromJSON("http://quora.christopher.su/questions/If-space-is-3-dimensional-can-time-als
o-be-3-dimensional")
$answer_count
[1] 7

$answer_wiki
[1] "<div class=\"hidden\" id=\"answer_wiki\"><div id=\"1d_ouhbnu_4206\"><div id=\"__w2_
EdwfLIZ_wiki\"></div></div></div>"

$question_details
[1] "<div class=\"question_details_text inline_editor_content\"></div>"

$question_text
[1] "If space is 3-dimensional, can time also be 3-dimensional?"

$topics
[1] "Science, Engineering, and Technology" "Science"
[3] "Physical Sciences"                    "Physics"
[5] "Theoretical Physics"

$want_answers
[1] 9
```

Due to recent changes in the Quora API, some of the preceding URLs might be broken. Moreover, Quora is not very open with the unofficial APIs. Hence, please refer to the API provided by Quora at `http://www.quora.com/Edmond-Lau/Edmond-Laus-Posts/Quora-Extension-API`.

> The preceding URL provides the API that would retrieve the data of the currently logged in user. This official API provides data such as the name, the Quora URL, number of unread messages, and some of the notifications. With more social networks becoming open to the API, I believe that Quora might soon provide official API access.

Mapping solutions using Google Maps

Google Maps provides mapping solutions. By using the R package `RgoogleMaps`, we can get the static images from Google Maps using the name of the place or using the latitude and longitude of that place. We can also use the map as the background and plot location-specific charts.

In this section, we will see how to access the Google Maps API from R. We need to first install the package `RgoogleMaps`:

```
install.packages("RgoogleMaps")
library(RgoogleMaps)
```

We can use the function `getGeoCode` to get the exact latitude and longitude of a specific place. We will get the latitude and the longitude of some of the most famous places. The code is as follows:

```
getGeoCode("Big Ben")
getGeoCode("10 Downing Street")
getGeoCode("London Eye")
```

We get the following output:

```
> getGeoCode("Big Ben")
      lat        lon
51.5007292 -0.1246254
> getGeoCode("10 Downing Street")
      lat        lon
51.5033635 -0.1276248
> getGeoCode("London Eye")
     lat       lon
51.503324 -0.119543
```

We can get the static maps for the preceding places using the function `GetMap`. Let's look at London's iconic timepiece on a map:

```
BigBenMap<- GetMap(center="Big Ben", zoom=13)
PlotOnStaticMap(BigBenMap)
```

We get the following output:

We can also plot multiple locations on the map. Now, let's plot all of the preceding locations with colored markers to identify their locations. We will store the latitude and longitude in a numeric vector and make the mean of all three, the center of the map. After setting the zoom level, we can plot the map using the same function GetMap. We use the parameter markers to mark the points of the locations. The code is as follows:

```
lat = c(51.5007292,51.5033635,51.503324);
lon = c(-0.1246254,-0.1276248,-0.119543);
center = c(mean(lat), mean(lon));
zoom<- min(MaxZoom(range(lat), range(lon)));
Map <- GetMap(center=center, zoom=zoom,markers =
paste0("&markers=color:blue|label:B|",
"51.5007292,-0.1246254&markers=color:green|label:D|51.5033635,
-0.1276248&markers=",
"color:red|color:red|label:L|51.503324,-0.119543"),
destfile = "MyTile1.png");
PlotOnStaticMap(Map)
```

We get the following output:

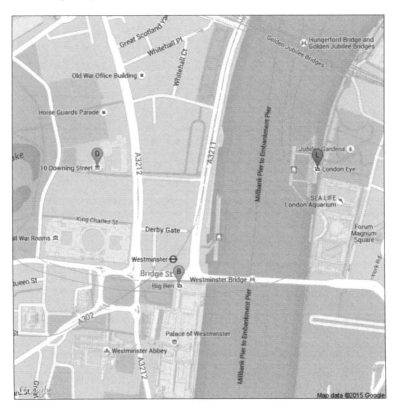

We will use the data that we created in *Chapter 4, Finding Popular Photos on Instagram*. In that chapter, we extracted the data on the number of comments and likes from various users with their geographical location whenever it was enabled. In order to create the data, that is `geodata`, we considered the data that had a geo-location and filtered out the top 150 records based on the number of comments. Let's use the data to plot on the map. The code is as follows:

```
geodata<- read.csv("geodata.csv")
head(geodata)
```

We get the following output:

```
> head(geodata)
   longitude latitude comments_count
1 -117.42232 33.22396           4982
2 -118.37042 34.09666           4976
3 -117.15942 32.70849           4800
4 -119.97915 39.08244           3318
5 -118.37493 34.09985           2938
6   15.33974 37.95571           2630
```

We compute the mean to mark the center of the map and then we use the function `GetMap` to get the map along with the specified parametric settings. In order to create the bubble chart on the map, we use the function `bubbleMap` and pass the map and the dataset as the parameter. Thus, the bubble chart can be plotted:

```
center = c(mean(geodata$latitude), mean(geodata$longitude));
map<- GetMap(center=center,
zoom=3,
size=c(480,480),
destfile = file.path(tempdir(),"meuse.png"),
maptype="mobile",
SCALE = 1);
par(cex=1)
```

We can change the zoom level by tuning the zoom parameter, and the size of the bubble can be changed using the `cex` parameter. Note that the output covers only a fraction of the complete plotting; by adjusting the zoom level, the complete geography can be covered. The code is as follows:

```
bubbleMap(geodata
coords = c("longitude", "latitude"),
map=map,
zcol='comments_count',
key.entries = 100+ 100 * 2^(0:4));
```

We get the following output:

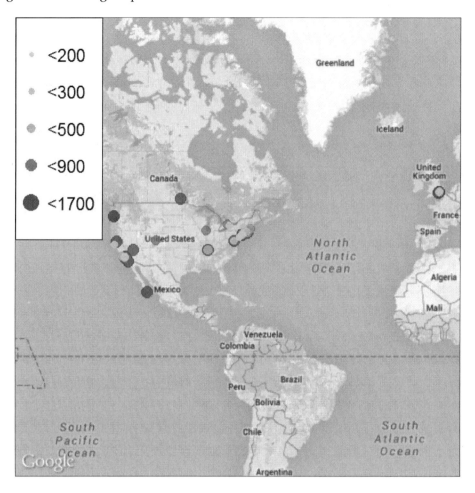

The package RgoogleMaps allows multiple functions to make the map look different; print text at various geographic locations on the map, plot charts keeping a specific location's map as the background image, and much more. Have a look at the various functions offered through this package in R at https://cran.r-project.org/web/packages/RgoogleMaps/RgoogleMaps.pdf.

We can also visualize the spatial data and models on top of Google Maps using the other popular packages in R. Refer to the documentation of the package at https://cran.r-project.org/web/packages/ggmap/ggmap.pdf.

The Google Maps API has a limit of 2,500 requests per day.

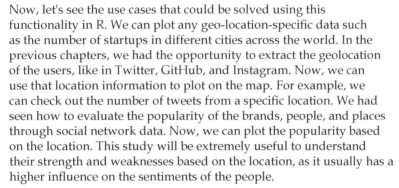

Exercise

Now, let's see the use cases that could be solved using this functionality in R. We can plot any geo-location-specific data such as the number of startups in different cities across the world. In the previous chapters, we had the opportunity to extract the geolocation of the users, like in Twitter, GitHub, and Instagram. Now, we can use that location information to plot on the map. For example, we can check out the number of tweets from a specific location. We had seen how to evaluate the popularity of the brands, people, and places through social network data. Now, we can plot the popularity based on the location. This study will be extremely useful to understand their strength and weaknesses based on the location, as it usually has a higher influence on the sentiments of the people.

The exercise would be to pull the location data for the top users in Instagram and then plot the number of users across the world.

Professional network data from LinkedIn

LinkedIn is a social networking website for people in professional jobs. It has over 364 million users across the world. Many companies have started using LinkedIn to publish their job requirements and as a medium to showcase their skillset to the world.

In order to access the LinkedIn data, we need to use the package Rlinkedin. Get the latest package from the GitHub repository using the following code:

```
install_github("mpiccirilli/Rlinkedin")
library(Rlinkedin)
```

For authentication, we need to have a LinkedIn app. It can be registered at https://www.linkedin.com/developer/apps. Similar to the way we had created an app in Facebook, Instagram, and GitHub, we need to create an app at LinkedIn as well. Once the app is created, it will appear in your developers login.

Please refer to the following screenshot to know what it looks like:

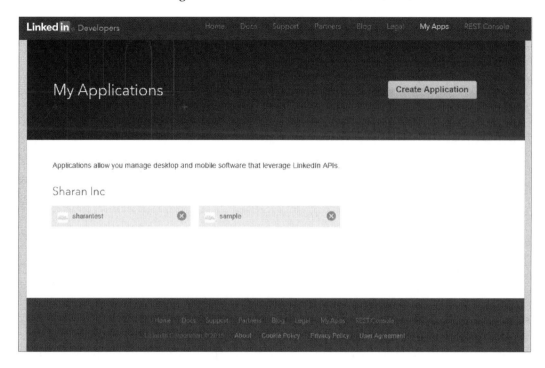

The details of the app, such as the client ID and client secret can be found by clicking and opening the app. After creating the app and specifying the redirect URL, we can go ahead with the authentication using the following code:

```
app_name<- "Enter your App name here"
consumer_key<- " Enter your client ID here "
consumer_secret<- " Enter your client secret here "
in.auth<- inOAuth(app_name, consumer_key, consumer_secret)
```

The preceding code will initiate the authentication; it will open a new window in the browser and request the following permissions:

Once the permissions are granted, the authentication will be completed. The LinkedIn API is used to provide all the information about our network such as the connections, profile information about the user, their first degree connections, search for companies based on the keywords or location, and much more. But with the latest changes in the way the API operated, only some of the basic details are available to all the users whereas most of the vital information is available only to the partners.

The only detail that can be now downloaded is your own basic profile, and you can search about a company or get their basic details. This can be implemented using the function searchCompanies. The following code retrieves the details of six different companies, including the LinkedIn Corporation:

```
search.comp<- searchCompanies(in.auth, keywords = "LinkedIn")
head(search.comp)
```

We get the following output:

```
> head(search.comp)
[[1]]
[[1]]$company_id
[1] "1337"

[[1]]$company_name
[1] "LinkedIn"

[[1]]$universal_name
[1] "linkedin"

[[1]]$website
[1] "http://www.linkedin.com"

[[1]]$twitter_handle
[1] "linkedin"

[[1]]$employee_count
[1] "5001-10000"

[[1]]$company_status
[1] "operating"

[[1]]$founded
[1] "2003"

[[1]]$num_followers
[1] "1355985"

[[1]]$description
[1] "Founded in 2003, LinkedIn connects the world's professionals to make them more prod
uctive and successful. With more than 380 million members worldwide, including executive
s from every Fortune 500 company, LinkedIn is the world's largest professional network o
n the Internet. The company has a diversified business model with revenue coming from Ta
lent Solutions, Marketing Solutions and Premium Subscriptions products. Headquartered in
 Silicon Valley, LinkedIn has offices across the globe."
```

In order to get your basic profile, you can use the function getProfile. This function will return details such as the name, location, designation, industry, number of connections, a brief description about the current position, and start date of the current position. When you set the parameter connections to TRUE, the access request will be rejected as the API doesn't allow public access to the connection details.

The code is as follows:

```
getProfile(token = in.auth, connections = FALSE, id = NULL)
```

We get the following output:

```
> getProfile(token = in.auth, connections = FALSE, id = NULL)
[[1]]
[[1]]$connection_id
[1] "WtLQt8zNmc"

[[1]]$fname
[1] "Sharan Kumar"

[[1]]$lname
[1] "R"

[[1]]$formatted_name
[1] "Sharan Kumar R"

[[1]]$location
[1] "Bengaluru Area, India"

[[1]]$headline
[1] "Lead Business Analyst (Analytics) at FreeCharge - India's leading website for onli
ne recharge"

[[1]]$industry
[1] "Information Technology and Services"

[[1]]$num_connections
[1] "500"

[[1]]$profile_url
[1] "https://www.linkedin.com/in/rsharankumar"

[[1]]$num_positions
[1] 1

[[1]]$position1_id
[1] "656569490"
```

Even though LinkedIn has blocked most of its API to the public, you can still get access by getting into the partnership program. You can sign in for a partnership program by going to https://developer.linkedin.com/partner-programs.

By signing into the partnership program, you get access to additional API functionalities as well as increased call limits with support. There are multiple programs based on the relevance and the requirements, you can request for a suitable program.

Getting Blogger data

Blogger is a blog publishing service that was bought by Google in the year 2003 and it has more than 500,000 blogs. Blogger provides numerous APIs to access the data, provided you have the API key and know some required data such as the blog ID, user ID, and post ID based on the data that you are trying to access.

In order to get the API key, one has to create a project in the Google developer's console. Here's the screenshot of the Google developer's console:

On opening the console, create a new project, open it and click on the link **APIs &auth**, select the credential, look to see if any client IDs and client keys are available, and if not then create one. On creation, you will be provided with a client ID and an API key that can be used to access the data.

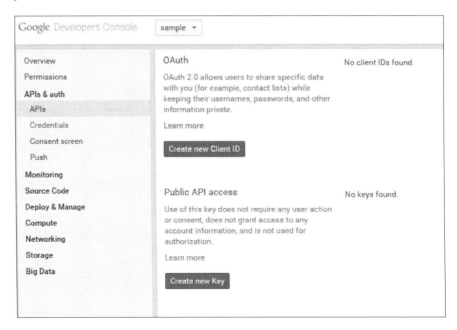

To know about the various data that can be accessed, visit `https://developers.` `google.com/apis-explorer/#p/blogger/v3/`. This link has a list of services. Let's check out a few to understand how it would work.

First, let's try to get the number of blog posts. Click on the service **blogger.blogs.get** and provide the relevant details, as shown in the following screenshot:

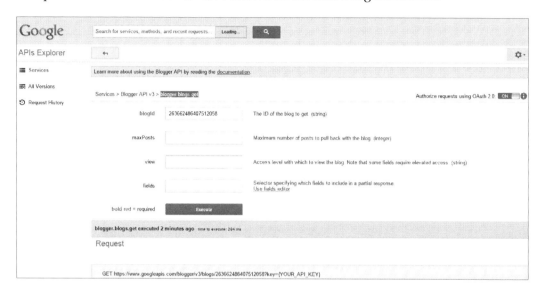

The preceding window shows the actual request URL and the response in the JSON format. We can now take the request URL and make the request from the R environment using the function `fromJSON`:

```
fromJSON("https://www.googleapis.com/blogger/v3/blogs/
263662486407512058?key=<Paste your API key here>")
```

We get the following output:

```
> fromJSON("https://www.googleapis.com/blogger/v3/blogs/263662486407512058?key=

$kind
[1] "blogger#blog"

$id
[1] "263662486407512058"

$name
[1] "Demystifying Data"

$description
[1] ""

$published
[1] "2014-05-29T01:39:06+05:30"

$updated
[1] "2015-04-29T23:46:03+05:30"

$url
[1] "http://blog.rsharankumar.com/"

$selfLink
[1] "https://www.googleapis.com/blogger/v3/blogs/263662486407512058"

$posts
$posts$totalItems
[1] 8

$posts$selfLink
[1] "https://www.googleapis.com/blogger/v3/blogs/263662486407512058/posts"


$pages
$pages$totalItems
[1] 0
```

The user doesn't need to be authenticated in order to retrieve the public blog post, but they will be required to provide the API key. However, in order to retrieve the private content, it is necessary to include the authorization HTTP header in the request. We can also monitor the number of requests made at the developer's console.

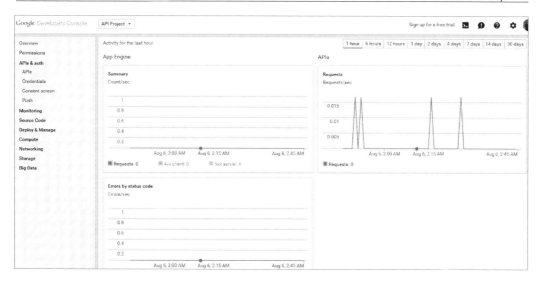

This API provides functionality to, not only retrieve the data from the blog, but also update a blog, publish a blog post that is on the draft, delete a blog post, search for keywords across the blogs, get a user profile, approve a comment, and numerous other things. To learn about the Blogger API usage, visit `https://developers.google.com/blogger/docs/3.0/using`.

Retrieving venue data from Foursquare

Foursquare is a local search services company that offers its service on the mobile platform as well as a website. Log in to Foursquare as a developer in order to get the idea of the API request and response patterns. On registering, a unique OAuth token is generated.

In the developer's login, open the explorer from the list of links on the left-hand side panel. Here's a screenshot of the developer's landing page:

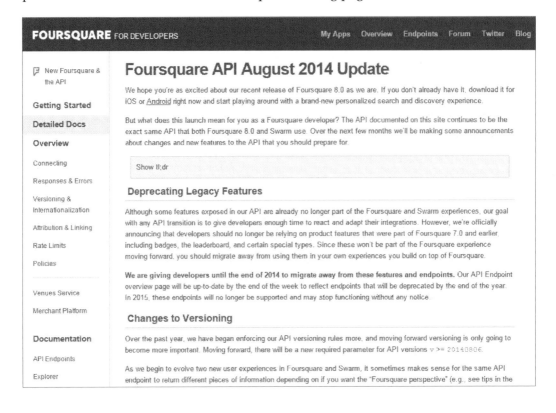

In the explorer panel, we can see how the request is being sent, which can again be replicated in R using either the function `fromJSON` or `GET`. The data will be retrieved in the JSON format. Here's the screenshot of the explorer panel:

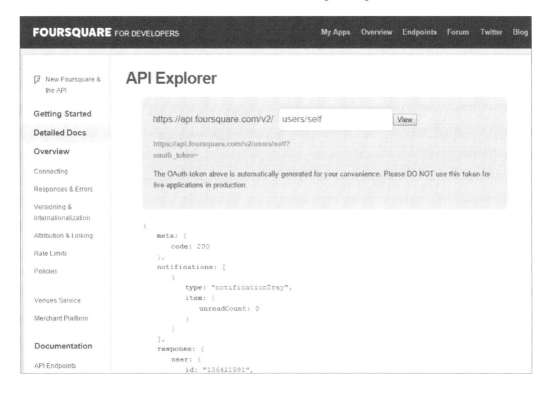

We can now execute the API request from R using the function `fromJSON`. First, let's get the user details:

```
fromJSON("https://api.foursquare.com/v2/users/
self?oauth_token=<Paste your OAuth token here>")
```

We get the following output:

```
$meta
code
 200

$notifications
$notifications[[1]]
$notifications[[1]]$type
[1] "notificationTray"

$notifications[[1]]$item
unreadCount
          0




$response
$response$user
$response$user$id
[1] "136421991"

$response$user$firstName
[1] "Sharan Kumar"

$response$user$lastName
[1] "R"

$response$user$gender
[1] "male"

$response$user$relationship
[1] "self"

$response$user$photo
                    prefix                              suffix
"https://irs0.4sqi.net/img/user/" "/136421991-4NZDODMVMKD1PHDA.jpg"
```

The preceding API request provides many details about the user such as name, location, check-ins, groups, badges, follower counts, and much more.

Next, we will use the functionality to extract details about a location. The following API requests complete details about the specified venue such as the name, address, contact number, latitude and longitude, ratings, venue's category, user count, tip count, visit count, price tier, currency accepted, likes, about our friends' visits and their tips, restaurant timings, and facilities provided. The code is as follows:

```
fromJSON("https://api.foursquare.com/v2/venues/
40a55d80f964a52020f31ee3?oauth_token=<Paste your OAuth token here>")
```

We get the following output:

```
$response$venue$name
[1] "Clinton St. Baking Co. & Restaurant'

$response$venue$contact
$response$venue$contact$phone
[1] "+16466026263"

$response$venue$contact$formattedPhone
[1] "+1 646-602-6263"


$response$venue$location
$response$venue$location$address
[1] "4 Clinton St"

$response$venue$location$crossStreet
[1] "at E Houston St"

$response$venue$location$lat
[1] 40.72108

$response$venue$location$lng
[1] -73.98394

$response$venue$location$postalCode
[1] "10002"

$response$venue$location$cc
[1] "US"

$response$venue$location$city
[1] "New York"

$response$venue$location$state
[1] "NY"

$response$venue$location$country
```

Other details that could be obtained here are the venues, various tips data, or basic details about the users who gave those tips, how many of those tips were liked, and so on. In the URL `https://api.foursquare.com/v2/venues/514d613de4b0ab03fe0601fb/tips?oauth_token=<Paste your OAuth token here>`, the following code identifies the venue `514d613de4b0ab03fe0601fb`. Here's the API request that would provide the required details:

```
fromJSON("https://api.foursquare.com/v2/venues/
514d613de4b0ab03fe0601fb/tips?oauth_token=<Paste your OAuth
token here>")
```

We get the following output:

```
                          id   createdAt
1  516d71a0498eb95100ce5d54  1366127008
2  555cbeaf498e363a1bf1e02e  1432141487
3  53d39d3b498e81b830540285  1406377275
4  526255a411d23ef7ee99a978  1382176164
5  51cafb50498e4603fd7ceedc  1372257104
                                                       text type
1                                          Amazing Coffee !!! user
2        The chocolates éclair is brilliant. Probably the best in town. user
3 The place is so elegant <U+2764><U+FE0F> Rainbow Pastry is a must. user
4                           Nutella crepes and red velvet is awesome user
5                          The Red Velvet cupcake is a must-try! user
                                          canonicalUrl lang likes.count
1 https://foursquare.com/item/516d71a0498eb95100ce5d54   en           1
2 https://foursquare.com/item/555cbeaf498e363a1bf1e02e   en           0
3 https://foursquare.com/item/53d39d3b498e81b830540285   en           0
4 https://foursquare.com/item/526255a411d23ef7ee99a978   en           0
5 https://foursquare.com/item/51cafb50498e4603fd7ceedc   en           0

          likes.groups
1 others, 1, 23258628, Pankaj S, Sharma, male, https://irs2.4sqi.net/img/user/, /2325
8-LNEV2LUYS0AYN0Z4.jpg
2
               NULL
3
               NULL
4
               NULL
5
               NULL
   likes.summary  like logView count  user.id user.firstName user.lastName user.gender
1       1 like FALSE    TRUE     0 23258628        Pankaj S        Sharma        male
2        <NA> FALSE    TRUE     0  6266673            Yash         Sinha        male
3        <NA> FALSE    TRUE     0 46943220         Aayushi          Shaw      female
4        <NA> FALSE    TRUE     0 57823908           Faraz        Sarwar        male
5        <NA> FALSE    TRUE     0 24713636         Vatsala         Jalan      female
           user.photo.prefix              user.photo.suffix
1 https://irs2.4sqi.net/img/user/ /23258628-LNEV2LUYS0AYN0Z4.jpg
```

We can drill down one more level to know more about an individual tip. Each tip will have a unique ID and we can use this ID to get the details of a tip. The request would provide us with the details about the tip. In the following URL, the following code identifies the tip `49f083e770c603bbe81f8eb4`:

```
fromJSON("https://api.foursquare.com/v2/tips/
49f083e770c603bbe81f8eb4?oauth_token=<Paste your OAuth token
here>")
```

We get the following output:

```
$response
$response$tip
$response$tip$id
[1] "49f083e770c603bbe81f8eb4"

$response$tip$createdAt
[1] 1240499175

$response$tip$text
[1] "for DINNER, not brunch, and get the fried chicken and blueberry pancakes. No wait,
and you get both meals in one."

$response$tip$type
[1] "user"

$response$tip$canonicalUrl
[1] "https://foursquare.com/item/49f083e770c603bbe81f8eb4"

$response$tip$lang
[1] "en"

$response$tip$likes
$response$tip$likes$count
[1] 5

$response$tip$likes$groups
    type count
1 others      5


  items
1 6111433, 535596, Tania, Jeff, Garcia, Thibodeau, female, male, https://irs3.4sqi.net/i
mg/user/, https://irs2.4sqi.net/img/user/, /2NS013ERBO22GOTF.jpg, /535596-SQDYQCJC415XQ5
CB.jpg
```

These are the various levels of details that could be obtained using the API of Foursquare. In order to know more about the API provided by Foursquare, visit `https://developer.foursquare.com/docs/`.

Use cases

This enormous amount of data could be very powerful. Some of the use cases possible include details such as the items that are most liked by the user based on mining the user's tips, performing correlations between different venues and getting to know more about the most similar venues, and, based on the likes data, we can also provide recommendations using collaborative filtering. Based on the venue data, we can also compute the clusters.

There are few more use cases that would help the venues, such as finding out the performance of a venue in terms of likes and positive tips from user, and comparing it with other nearby venues in the same category. Mining the text data would help the venues in knowing the areas of improvement. With exploration of the data, we can also get to know about the services that are most valued by the customers. This would help the venues in improving their rating.

Yelp and other networks

Yelp is a crowdsourced local business review and social networking site. Over 31 million people access Yelp's website each month. Getting the data from Yelp is quite similar to how we get it from the other social networks. The steps are as follows:

1. First, log in as a developer.
2. Then, register and get the authentication credentials.
3. Get the standard API request URL.
4. Pass the URL along with the authentication credentials to either the function `fromJSON` or `GET`.
5. Data will be retrieved in the JSON format.
6. Read the required data and convert it to data frame for further analysis.

To know about the various API services offered by Yelp, visit `https://www.yelp.com/developers/documentation/v2/overview`.

Websites such as Glassdoor and Indeed provide API access on request. The process involved in working with those APIs would be similar to those we have covered so far.

Limitations

The only limitation in performing social media mining is that the APIs consistently undergo changes with respect to the accessibility of the data and also in the way in which they work. Using the LinkedIn API, users were able to download the complete information about their network, but later it was made *on request*. Similarly, the Facebook API went through lot of changes too. When the data is accessed through the R package, the user needs to update. Alternatively, when accessed using the URL in the function `fromJSON`, then the API needs to be updated.

The other limitation is on the quality of the data. Since all this data is created by people online, there is always a possibility for skewness in the data. Therefore, measures should be taken to keep a check on the quality.

Summary

In this chapter, we saw how to access many of the social media websites and also discussed the various use cases that could be implemented. The methodology involved in accessing data through the APIs are similar to one another; while most APIs require authentication, some APIs can be accessed without authentication even in a browser. Most APIs provide the data in the JSON format, but for some popular sites there are packages built in R that can convert the data to a data frame while retrieving. This helps in speeding up the analysis. These APIs provide us the data in a variety of formats: structured in some cases, but unstructured in most cases. With a higher limit on the API requests that can be called, the volume at which we can generate data is also quite high.

In this book, we covered the methodologies to access the data from R using the APIs of various social media sites such as Twitter, Facebook, Instagram, GitHub, Foursquare, LinkedIn, Blogger, and a few more networks. This book also provided details on the implementation of various use cases using R programming. Now, you should be completely equipped to embark on your journey as a social media analyst.

Index

A

active users
  used, for building heterogeneous
    dataset 142, 143
additional metrics
  building 145-147
app
  creating, on Facebook platform 56, 57
  creating, on GitHub 136-138
avatar 193

B

Betweenness 67
Blogger 208
Blogger API usage
  URL 211
Blogger data
  obtaining 208-211
  URL 209
business cases
  defining 132, 172
  implementing 90

C

celebrity users and location hashtags
  reference 132
challenges, social media mining
  Big Data 5
  evaluation dilemma 6
  noise removal error 5
  sufficiency 5
Click-through rate (CTR) 56
closeness 68

cluster 68
clustering 118
clustering analysis
  reference 132
community detection
  via clustering 18
correlation analysis, EDA
  correlation, between languages 166-168
  correlation, on segmented data 165, 166
  correlation, with local regression
    curve 164, 165
  correlation, with regression line 163
  defining 161, 162
  references 171, 172
  trend of correlation, obtaining 168-170
  watchers, relating to forks 162, 163
CTR performance
  measuring, for page 77-80
**customer relationship
    management (CRM) 3**

D

data
  accessing, from Quora 196-198
  accessing, from R 97
  retrieving, from Wikipedia 181-190
data access
  comments, obtaining 102, 103
  followers, obtaining 100
  hashtag, using 104
  public media, searching from specific
    location 98
  public media, searching for
    specific hashtag 97

Thank you for buying
Mastering Social Media Mining with R

About Packt Publishing

Packt, pronounced 'packed', published its first book, *Mastering phpMyAdmin for Effective MySQL Management*, in April 2004, and subsequently continued to specialize in publishing highly focused books on specific technologies and solutions.

Our books and publications share the experiences of your fellow IT professionals in adapting and customizing today's systems, applications, and frameworks. Our solution-based books give you the knowledge and power to customize the software and technologies you're using to get the job done. Packt books are more specific and less general than the IT books you have seen in the past. Our unique business model allows us to bring you more focused information, giving you more of what you need to know, and less of what you don't.

Packt is a modern yet unique publishing company that focuses on producing quality, cutting-edge books for communities of developers, administrators, and newbies alike. For more information, please visit our website at www.packtpub.com.

About Packt Open Source

In 2010, Packt launched two new brands, Packt Open Source and Packt Enterprise, in order to continue its focus on specialization. This book is part of the Packt Open Source brand, home to books published on software built around open source licenses, and offering information to anybody from advanced developers to budding web designers. The Open Source brand also runs Packt's Open Source Royalty Scheme, by which Packt gives a royalty to each open source project about whose software a book is sold.

Writing for Packt

We welcome all inquiries from people who are interested in authoring. Book proposals should be sent to author@packtpub.com. If your book idea is still at an early stage and you would like to discuss it first before writing a formal book proposal, then please contact us; one of our commissioning editors will get in touch with you.

We're not just looking for published authors; if you have strong technical skills but no writing experience, our experienced editors can help you develop a writing career, or simply get some additional reward for your expertise.

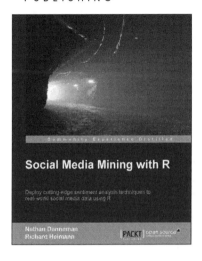

Social Media Mining with R

ISBN: 978-1-78328-177-0   Paperback: 122 pages

Deploy cutting-edge sentiment analysis techniques to real-world social media data using R

1. Learn how to face the challenges of analyzing social media data.

2. Get hands-on experience with the most common, up-to-date sentiment analysis tools and apply them to data collected from social media websites through a series of in-depth case studies, which includes how to mine Twitter data.

3. A focused guide to help you achieve practical results when interpreting social media data.

Learning Data Mining with R

ISBN: 978-1-78398-210-3   Paperback: 314 pages

Develop key skills and techniques with R to create and customize data mining algorithms

1. Develop a sound strategy for solving predictive modeling problems using the most popular data mining algorithms.

2. Gain understanding of the major methods of predictive modeling.

3. Packed with practical advice and tips to help you get to grips with data mining.

Please check **www.PacktPub.com** for information on our titles

R for Data Science

ISBN: 978-1-78439-086-0   Paperback: 364 pages

Learn and explore the fundamentals of data science with R

1. Familiarize yourself with R programming packages and learn how to utilize them effectively.

2. Learn how to detect different types of data mining sequences.

3. A step-by-step guide to understanding R scripts and the ramifications of your changes.

Instant Social Media Marketing with HootSuite

ISBN: 978-1-84969-666-1   Paperback: 60 pages

Manage and enhance your social media marketing with HootSuite

1. Learn something new in an Instant! A short, fast, focused guide delivering immediate results.

2. Presents you with an insight into your organization's social assets.

3. Packed with useful tips to automate your social media sharing and tracking.

4. Analyze social media traffic and generate reports using HootSuite.

Please check **www.PacktPub.com** for information on our titles

16350880R00138